Finest Recipe
Collection

PUBLICATIONS INTERNATIONAL, LTD.

Pictured on front cover (*clockwise from top*): Napoleons (*page 64*), Almond Cheesecake with Raspberries
(*page 78*), Swordfish with Leek Cream (*page 46*) and Seafood Ravioli with Fresh Tomato Sauce (*page 22*).

Pictured on back cover (*clockwise from top*): Banana Berry Brownie Pizza (*page 58*), Cherry Cream
Cheese Coffeecake (*page 30*), Pasta Tossed with Blue Cheese Sauce (*page 46*) and Southwestern
Cheesecake (*page 16*).

This edition published by Publications International, Ltd., 7373 North Cicero Avenue, Lincolnwood, Illinois
60646.

Manufactured in U.S.A.

8   7   6   5   4   3   2   1

ISBN: 1-56173-794-1

Microwave ovens vary in wattage and power output; cooking times given with microwave directions in this
publication may need to be adjusted. Consult manufacturer's instructions for suitable microwave-safe
cooking dishes.

Contents

A Word About PHILLY

PHILADELPHIA BRAND Cream Cheese Products... for the way we live today.

American moms and other great chefs have been baking, cooking and entertaining with PHILADELPHIA BRAND Cream Cheese for generations and PHILLY Cream Cheese is still America's favorite! It's the perfect ingredient for a variety of foods from appetizers and side dishes to main meal fare and desserts. PHILLY Cream Cheese products add a real touch of elegance to even the simplest of recipes.

The versatility of PHILLY Cream Cheese products makes them a natural for today's cooking. The smooth creamy texture can be spread, blended, melted, baked, cooked or simply topped on your favorite dish. And today you'll find PHILLY Cream Cheese products in a variety of convenient forms to fit all your needs. You know that PHILADELPHIA BRAND Cream Cheese brick has always been ideal for baking and cooking. But did you know that you can substitute Light PHILADELPHIA BRAND Neufchatel Cheese brick in your recipes and still get that creamy delicious taste with 33% less fat?

Although it was developed to be and is most often used as a spreading cheese, PHILADELPHIA BRAND Soft Cream Cheese is suitable for many recipes. You'll especially like the easy blending qualities of PHILLY Cream Cheese when preparing quick chilled recipes such as dips, spreads, frostings, cold sauces or fillings. In recipes calling for brick cream cheese, soft cream cheese should not be substituted because a softer consistency may result.

Whatever the occasion, PHILLY Cream Cheese products help make the most of it!

1/2 THE CALORIES
OF BUTTER OR MARGARINE

Soft
PHILADELPHIA
BRAND
PASTEURIZED **CREAM CHEESE**
WITH **CHIVES & ONION**
K

NET WT. 8 OZS.
(227g)

ALL NATURAL
FLAVORS

1/2 THE CALORIES
OF BUTTER OR MARGARINE

Soft
PHILADELPHIA
BRAND
PASTEURIZED **CREAM CHEESE**
WITH **SMOKED SALMON**
K

NET WT. 8 OZS.
(227g)

ALL NATURAL
FLAVORS

1/2 THE CALORIES
OF BUTTER OR MARGARINE

Soft
PHILADELPHIA
BRAND
PASTEURIZED **CREAM CHEESE**
WITH **HERB & GARLIC**
K

NET WT. 8 OZS.
(227g)

ALL NATURAL
FLAVORS

As always, 1/2 the calories of butter or margarine
PHILADELPHIA
BRAND
CREAM CHEESE
PASTEURIZED
KRAFT

As always,
1/2 the calories
of butter or margarine

Soft
PHILADELPHIA
BRAND
CREAM CHEESE
PASTEURIZED
KRAFT

1/2 THE CALORIES
OF BUTTER OR MARGARINE

Soft
PHILADELPHIA
BRAND
PASTEURIZED **CREAM CHEESE**
WITH **OLIVE & PIMENTO**
K

NET WT. 8 OZS.
(227g)

ALL NATURAL
FLAVORS

1/2 THE CALORIES
OF BUTTER OR MARGARINE

Soft
PHILADELPHIA
BRAND
PASTEURIZED **CREAM CHEESE**
WITH **PINEAPPLE**

NET WT. 8 OZS.
(227g)

ALL NATURAL
FLAVORS

1/2 THE CALORIES
OF BUTTER OR MARGARINE

Soft
PHILADELPHIA
BRAND
PASTEURIZED **CREAM CHEESE**
WITH **STRAWBERRIES**
K

NET WT. 8 OZS.
(227g)

ALL NATURAL
FLAVORS

THREE–PEPPER QUESADILLAS

For extra convenience, assemble these quesadillas in advance.

> 1 cup thin green pepper strips
> 1 cup thin red pepper strips
> 1 cup thin yellow pepper strips
> ½ cup thin onion slices
> ⅓ cup PARKAY Margarine
> ½ teaspoon ground cumin
> 1 (8 oz.) pkg. PHILADELPHIA BRAND Cream Cheese, softened
> 1 (8 oz.) pkg. KRAFT Shredded Sharp Cheddar Cheese
> ½ cup (2 ozs.) KRAFT 100% Grated Parmesan Cheese
> 10 (6-inch) flour tortillas

- Preheat oven to 425°.
- Sauté peppers and onions in margarine in large skillet. Stir in cumin. Drain, reserving liquid.
- Beat cheeses in small mixing bowl at medium speed with electric mixer until well blended.
- Spoon 2 tablespoons cheese mixture onto each tortilla; top with pepper mixture. Fold tortillas in half; place on baking sheet. Brush with reserved liquid.
- Bake 10 minutes. Cut each tortilla into thirds. Serve warm with salsa.

2½ dozen

Prep time: 20 minutes
Cooking time: 10 minutes

Tip: To make ahead, prepare as directed except for baking. Cover; refrigerate. When ready to serve, bake at 425°, 15 to 20 minutes or until thoroughly heated.

HOT CHEESY ALMOND SPREAD

You may want to double the recipe for any appetizer party… this favorite disappears rapidly!

> 1 (8 oz.) pkg. PHILADELPHIA BRAND Cream Cheese, softened
> 1½ cups (6 ozs.) KRAFT Shredded Swiss Cheese
> ⅓ cup KRAFT Real Mayonnaise
> ¼ cup chopped green onion
> ⅛ teaspoon ground nutmeg
> ⅛ teaspoon pepper
> ¼ cup sliced almonds, toasted

- Preheat oven to 350°.
- Beat all ingredients except almonds in small mixing bowl at medium speed with electric mixer until well blended. Stir in almonds. Spread into 9-inch pie plate.
- Bake 15 minutes, stirring after 8 minutes. Serve with assorted crackers or party rye bread slices.

2⅓ cups

Prep time: 15 minutes
Cooking time: 15 minutes

MICROWAVE: • Prepare recipe as directed except for baking. • Microwave on MEDIUM (50%) 6 minutes or until Swiss cheese is melted and mixture is warm, stirring after 4 minutes. (*Do not overcook.*) • Stir before serving. Garnish with additional toasted sliced almonds, if desired. Serve with assorted crackers or party rye bread slices.

Microwave cooking time: 6 minutes

Three-Pepper Quesadillas

PIZZA DIP

PHILLY Cream Cheese blended with Italian seasonings is the tasty base for this zesty dip.

    1 (8 oz.) pkg PHILADELPHIA BRAND
        Cream Cheese, softened
    1 teaspoon Italian seasoning
    ⅛ teaspoon garlic powder
    ½ cup pizza sauce
    ½ cup (2 ozs.) chopped pepperoni
    ¼ cup chopped green pepper
    1 (4 oz.) can mushroom pieces and
        stems, drained
    1 cup (4 ozs.) KRAFT Shredded Low-
        Moisture Part-Skim Mozzarella
        Cheese

• Preheat oven to 350°.
• Beat cream cheese and seasonings in
  small mixing bowl at medium speed with
  electric mixer until well blended. Spread
  onto bottom of 9-inch pie plate.
• Cover cream cheese mixture with pizza
  sauce; top with remaining ingredients.
• Bake 15 to 20 minutes or until mixture is
  thoroughly heated and cheese is melted.
  Serve with crackers.   *10 servings*

Prep time: 15 minutes
Cooking time: 20 minutes

BACON APPETIZER CRESCENTS

For extra convenience, prepare the filling in advance.

    1 (8 oz.) pkg. PHILADELPHIA
        BRAND Cream Cheese, softened
    8 OSCAR MAYER Bacon Slices,
        crisply cooked, crumbled
    ⅓ cup (1½ ozs.) KRAFT 100% Grated
        Parmesan Cheese
    ¼ cup finely chopped onion
    2 tablespoons chopped fresh parsley
    1 tablespoon milk
    2 (8 oz.) cans refrigerated quick
        crescent dinner rolls
    1 egg, beaten
    1 teaspoon cold water

• Preheat oven to 375°.
• Beat cream cheese, bacon, parmesan
  cheese, onion, parsley and milk in small
  mixing bowl at medium speed with
  electric mixer until well blended.
• Separate dough into eight rectangles;
  firmly press perforations together to seal.
  Spread each rectangle with 2 rounded
  measuring tablespoonfuls cream cheese
  mixture.
• Cut each rectangle in half diagonally;
  repeat with opposite corners. Cut in half
  crosswise to form six triangles. Fold points
  over cream cheese mixture.
• Place on greased cookie sheet; brush with
  combined egg and water. Sprinkle with
  poppy seeds, if desired.
• Bake 12 to 15 minutes or until golden
  brown. Serve immediately.
                Approximately 4 dozen

Prep time: 30 minutes
Cooking time: 15 minutes

8

Bacon Appetizer Crescents

SPA TORTILLAS

The combination of crunchy, fresh vegetables, PHILLY Cream Cheese and spicy seasonings is the filling for these tasty tortillas.

  1 (8 oz.) container Light
      PHILADELPHIA BRAND
      Pasteurized Process Cream Cheese
      Product
  2 teaspoons chili power
  1 teaspoon dried oregano leaves,
      crushed
  ½ teaspoon ground cumin
  ¼ teaspoon hot pepper sauce
  1 cup coarsely chopped tomato
  ½ cup coarsely chopped cucumber
  ½ cup small broccoli flowerets
  ½ cup coarsely chopped carrots
  ¼ cup green onion slices
  2 tablespoon chopped green pepper
  8 (6-inch) flour tortillas

- Preheat oven 325°.
- Stir together cream cheese product and seasonings in large bowl until well blended. Add vegetables; mix well.
- Wrap tortillas in foil. Bake 15 minutes.
- Spoon ⅓ cup vegetable mixture onto each tortilla; roll up. Serve with salsa, if desired.   *4 servings*

Prep time: 15 minutes
Cooking time: 15 minutes

CORONADO DIP

  2 (1 lb.) boneless, skinless chicken
      breasts, cut into 1-inch pieces
  ¾ cup cold water
  1 (1.5 oz.) envelope taco seasoning mix
  1 (8 oz.) pkg. Light PHILADELPHIA
      BRAND Neufchatel Cheese,
      softened
  1 tablespoon lime juice
  1 tablespoon skim milk
  ½ cup chopped tomato
  2 tablespoons shredded KRAFT Light
      Naturals Reduced Fat Sharp
      Cheddar Cheese
  2 tablespoons shredded KRAFT Light
      Naturals Reduced Fat Monterey
      Jack Cheese
  2 tablespoons green onion slices
  2 tablespoons chopped red pepper
  1 tablespoon chopped pitted ripe olives

- Bring chicken, water and taco seasoning mix to boil in large skillet; reduce heat. Cover; simmer 25 minutes.
- Cool slightly; shred chicken.
- Place neufchatel cheese, lime juice and milk in food processor or blender container; process until well blended.
- When ready to serve, spread neufchatel cheese mixture onto center of large serving plate; surround with chicken. Top with remaining ingredients. Serve with tortilla chips.   *12 servings*

Prep time: 25 minutes
Cooking time: 25 minutes

To shred chicken, pull cooked chicken breasts in opposite directions using two forks. Continue until chicken is desired shred size.

10

Coronado Dip

HAM & DIJON PASTRY CUPS

1 (17 ¼ oz.) pkg. frozen ready-to-bake puff pastry sheets, thawed
1 (8 oz.) container PHILADELPHIA BRAND Soft Cream Cheese with Chives & Onion
1 cup (4 ozs.) KRAFT Shredded Swiss Cheese
4 OSCAR MAYER Smoked Cooked Ham Slices, chopped
⅓ cup chopped red pepper
1 egg, beaten
2 tablespoons Dijon mustard

- Preheat oven to 425°.
- On lightly floured surface, roll puff pastry into two 12×9-inch rectangles. Cut each rectangle into twelve 3-inch squares.
- Place pastry squares, with pastry corners pointing up, in cups of medium-size muffin pan.
- Stir together remaining ingredients in medium bowl until well blended. Spoon 1 tablespoonful cheese mixture into each pastry cup.
- Bake 15 to 18 minutes or until pastry is golden brown. *2 dozen*

Prep time: 20 minutes
Cooking time: 18 minutes

12

CRISPY WONTONS WITH ORIENTAL DIPPING SAUCE

Sesame oil and Chinese rice wine add a unique blend of flavors to this recipe. To make ahead, wrap assembled wontons securely in plastic wrap and refrigerate until ready to bake.

½ lb. ground pork, cooked, well drained
1 (8 oz.) container PHILADELPHIA BRAND Soft Cream Cheese with Chives & Onion
1 teaspoon chopped peeled fresh ginger root
1 teaspoon sesame oil
32 wonton wrappers
Sesame seeds
Oriental Dipping Sauce

- Preheat oven to 425°.
- Mix together meat, cream cheese, ginger and sesame oil in medium bowl until well blended.
- Place 1 tablespoon meat mixture in center of each wonton wrapper. Bring corners together over meat mixture; twist. Pinch together to enclose meat in wonton wrapper. Flatten bottom. Repeat with remaining meat mixture and wonton wrappers.
- Place in 15×10×1-inch jelly roll pan. Brush lightly with water; sprinkle with sesame seeds.
- Bake 10 to 12 minutes or until golden brown. Remove from pan; drain on paper towels. Serve with Oriental Dipping Sauce. *32 appetizers*

ORIENTAL DIPPING SAUCE

2 tablespoons soy sauce
1 tablespoon Chinese rice wine
1 tablespoon cold water

- Stir together ingredients in small bowl until well blended.

Prep time: 25 minutes
Cooking time: 12 minutes

13

Crispy Wontons with Oriental Dipping Sauce

CHILLED MELON SOUP

With melons so plentiful in the summer, make double batches of this flavorful soup and store in the refrigerator for quick enjoyment.

> **1 (8 oz.) container PHILADELPHIA BRAND Soft Cream Cheese with Pineapple**
> **2 cups cantaloupe chunks**
> **1 cup honeydew melon chunks**
> **1 cup orange juice**
> **¼ teaspoon salt**

- Place ingredients in food processor or blender container; process until well blended. Chill.   *4 servings*

Prep time: 10 minutes plus chilling

PEPPERONI SPREAD

> **3 ozs. pepperoni**
> **¼ cup fresh parsley, stemmed**
> **1 (8 oz.) pkg. Light PHILADELPHIA BRAND Neufchatel Cheese, softened**
> **3 tablespoons skim milk**

- Place pepperoni and parsley in food processor or blender container; process until chopped.
- Add remaining ingredients; process until well blended. Serve with assorted vegetable dippers and bread sticks.   *1½ cups*

Prep time: 10 minutes

Variation: Substitute OSCAR MAYER Smoked Cooked Ham for pepperoni.

CHEESE & NUT LOG

Pistachios add flair to this great make-ahead recipe.

> **1½ cups (6 ozs.) KRAFT Shredded Sharp Cheddar Cheese**
> **4 ozs. PHILADELPHIA BRAND Cream Cheese, softened**
> **2 tablespoons finely chopped green onion**
> **2 tablespoons finely chopped red pepper**
> **1 small garlic clove, minced**
> **2 teaspoons white wine worcestershire sauce**
> **4 ozs. PHILADELPHIA BRAND Cream Cheese, softened**
> **½ cup (2 ozs.) KRAFT Blue Cheese Crumbles**
> **2 tablespoons milk**
> **⅓ cup finely chopped red or natural pistachio nuts**

- Beat cheddar cheese and 4 ounces cream cheese in small mixing bowl at medium speed with electric mixer until well blended. Add onions, peppers, garlic and worcestershire sauce; mix well. Chill 30 minutes.
- Beat remaining 4 ounces cream cheese, blue cheese and milk in small mixing bowl at medium speed with electric mixer until well blended.
- Shape cheddar cheese mixture into 8-inch log. Spread blue cheese mixture evenly over top and sides of log. Cover with pistachio nuts. Chill several hours.   *10 to 12 servings*

Prep time: 20 minutes plus chilling

SALAMI & CHEESE TOPPED PITA CHIPS

1 (8 oz.) container PHILADELPHIA BRAND Soft Cream Cheese
1 cup (4 ozs.) KRAFT Shredded Low-Moisture Part-Skim Mozzarella Cheese
½ cup chopped OSCAR MAYER Hard Salami Slices
1 small tomato, seeded, chopped
⅛ teaspoon pepper
  Toasted pita wedges

- Stir together cheeses, salami, tomatoes and pepper in medium bowl until well blended.
- Top each pita wedge with 1 rounded teaspoonful cheese mixture. Place on cookie sheet.
- Broil 3 to 4 minutes or until cheese is melted.   *Approximately 4 dozen*

Prep time: 10 minutes
Cooking time: 4 minutes

CLASSIC DIP

1 (8 oz.) container PHILADELPHIA BRAND Soft Cream Cheese
1 (0.6 oz.) envelope GOOD SEASONS Zesty Italian Salad Dressing Mix
1 (8 oz.) container plain yogurt
1 tablespoon milk

- Stir together ingredients in small bowl until well blended. Chill. Serve with assorted vegetable dippers.   *1 cup*

Prep time: 10 minutes plus chilling

OLÉ SPINACH DIP

Host an international buffet with appetizers from around the world. This creamy spinach dip is a natural accompaniment to other PHILLY Cream Cheese recipes such as Oriental Spread, Crispy Wontons with Oriental Dipping Sauce and Indonesian Satay, to name just a few.

1 (8 oz.) container PHILADELPHIA BRAND Soft Cream Cheese
¼ cup half and half
2 cups (8 ozs.) shredded CASINO Natural Monterey Jack Cheese with Jalapeño Peppers
1 (10 oz.) pkg. BIRDS EYE Chopped Spinach, thawed, well drained
½ cup chopped onion
½ cup chopped pitted ripe olives
1 tablespoon red wine vinegar
¼ teaspoon hot pepper sauce (optional)

- Preheat oven to 400°.
- Stir together cream cheese and half and half in medium bowl until well blended. Add remaining ingredients; mix well. Spread into 9-inch pie plate.
- Bake 20 to 25 minutes or until light golden brown. Serve with tortilla chips.
    10 to 12 servings

Prep time: 15 minutes
Cooking time: 25 minutes

SOUTHWESTERN CHEESECAKE

All of your favorite southwestern ingredients in a savory cheesecake... fantastic looking and tasting!

1 cup finely crushed tortilla chips
3 tablespoons PARKAY Margarine, melted
2 (8 oz.) pkgs. PHILADELPHIA BRAND Cream Cheese, softened
2 eggs
1 (8 oz.) pkg. KRAFT Shredded Colby/ Monterey Jack Cheese
1 (4 oz.) can chopped green chilies, drained
1 cup BREAKSTONE'S Sour Cream
1 cup chopped orange or yellow pepper
½ cup green onion slices
⅓ cup chopped tomatoes
¼ cup pitted ripe olive slices

- Preheat oven to 325°.
- Stir together chips and margarine in small bowl; press onto bottom of 9-inch springform pan. Bake 15 minutes.
- Beat cream cheese and eggs in large mixing bowl at medium speed with electric mixer until well blended. Mix in shredded cheese and chilies; pour over crust. Bake 30 minutes.
- Spread sour cream over cheesecake. Loosen cake from rim of pan; cool before removing rim of pan. Chill.
- Top with remaining ingredients just before serving.   *16 to 20 servings*

Prep time: 20 minutes plus chilling
Cooking time: 30 minutes

———————— ◆ ◆ ◆ ————————

To make an attractive design on top of this cheesecake, simply cut three diamonds out of paper. Place on top of cheesecake. Place green onion slices around diamonds. Remove cutouts; fill in with peppers. Add a strip of tomatoes down the center. Garnish with olives.

INDONESIAN SATAY

4 (approx. 2 lbs.) boneless, skinless chicken breasts, cut into strips
¼ cup lime juice
2 garlic cloves, minced
1 teaspoon grated lime peel
½ teaspoon ground ginger
½ teaspoon cayenne pepper
   Spicy Peanut Sauce

- Marinate chicken in lime juice, garlic, peel, ginger and pepper in refrigerator 1 hour.
- Prepare coals for grilling.
- Thread chicken on individual wooden skewers; place on greased grill over hot coals (coals will be glowing). Grill, uncovered, 3 to 5 minutes on each side or until tender. Serve with Spicy Peanut Sauce.   *15 servings*

SPICY PEANUT SAUCE

1 (8 oz.) pkg. PHILADELPHIA BRAND Cream Cheese, cubed
½ cup milk
3 tablespoons peanut butter
2 tablespoons packed brown sugar
½ teaspoon ground cardamom
⅛ teaspoon cayenne pepper

- Stir together ingredients in small saucepan over low heat until smooth.

Prep time: 20 minutes plus marinating
Cooking time: 10 minutes

Variation: Prepare chicken as directed except for grilling. Place skewers on rack of broiler pan. Broil 10 to 15 minutes or until tender, turning halfway through cooking time.

16

Indonesian Satay

PEPPERONCINI SPREAD

It's best to make this spread early in the day or even the day before your party so flavors can blend.

> 1 (8 oz.) container PHILADELPHIA BRAND Soft Cream Cheese
> ½ cup (2 ozs.) shredded provolone cheese
> ¼ cup (1 oz.) KRAFT 100% Grated Parmesan Cheese
> ⅛ teaspoon garlic powder
> 1 (12 oz.) jar pepperoncini, drained, stemmed, seeded, chopped
> 1 plum tomato, diced

- Stir together cheeses and garlic powder in medium bowl until well blended.
- Add pepperoncini and tomatoes; mix well. Chill. Garnish with fresh chives and green, red and yellow pepper cutouts, if desired. Serve with toasted bread cutouts.
  2½ cups

Prep time: 20 minutes plus chilling

◆◆◆

Cut bread slices with 2-inch cookie cutters. Bake at 325°, 5 minutes per side or until lightly toasted on both sides.

PIZZA ROLL

> 1 (1 lb.) loaf frozen Italian bread dough, thawed
> 1 (8 oz.) container PHILADELPHIA BRAND Soft Cream Cheese with Herb & Garlic
> 1½ cups (6 ozs.) KRAFT Shredded Low-Moisture Part-Skim Mozzarella Cheese
> ¾ cup (3 ozs.) chopped pepperoni
> ⅓ cup finely chopped green pepper
> 1 tablespoon olive oil
> ½ teaspoon Italian seasoning

- Roll dough to 15×10-inch rectangle on floured surface. Spread cream cheese over dough to within 1 inch of edges.
- Sprinkle mozzarella cheese, pepperoni and peppers over cream cheese. Roll up dough from long side; press edges together to seal. Brush top and sides with olive oil; sprinkle with seasoning.
- Cover; let rise in warm place 1 hour.
- Preheat oven to 350°.
- Bake 30 to 35 minutes or until golden brown.   *10 to 12 servings*

Prep time: 25 minutes plus rising
Cooking time: 35 minutes

HERB & GARLIC BITES

Finely chopped ham or crumbled, crisply cooked bacon, are delicious alternatives to pepperoni.

> 2 (7.5 oz.) cans refrigerated buttermilk biscuits
> 1 (8 oz.) container PHILADELPHIA BRAND Soft Cream Cheese with Herb & Garlic
> 6 ozs. pepperoni, finely chopped
> 1 egg, beaten

- Preheat oven to 400°.
- Separate each biscuit in half. Gently stretch dough to form 3-inch circles.
- Stir together cream cheese and pepperoni in small bowl until well blended. Spoon 1½ teaspoons cream cheese mixture onto center of each circle. Fold in half; press edges together to seal.
- Place on cookie sheet. Brush with egg. Bake 8 to 10 minutes or until golden brown. Serve immediately.
  Approximately 3½ dozen

Prep time: 10 minutes
Cooking time: 10 minutes

18

Pepperoncini Spread

SPINACH RICOTTA SPREAD

1 qt. chopped fresh spinach
½ cup chopped onion
1 (8 oz.) pkg. Light PHILADELPHIA
    BRAND Neufchatel Cheese,
    softened
¾ cup lowfat ricotta cheese
½ teaspoon dried basil leaves, crushed
½ teaspoon dried oregano leaves,
    crushed
¼ teaspoon salt
⅛ teaspoon garlic power
⅛ teaspoon pepper
¾ cup chopped tomato
2 tablespoons KRAFT 100% Grated
    Parmesan Cheese

- Preheat oven to 350°.
- Place spinach and onions in small
  saucepan. Cover; cook 5 minutes or until
  tender.
- Beat cheeses and seasonings in small
  mixing bowl at medium speed with
  electric mixer until well blended. Stir in
  spinach mixture; spread into 9-inch pie
  plate.
- Bake 15 to 20 minutes or until thoroughly
  heated. Top with remaining ingredients.
  Serve with crisp rye crackers or bagel
  chips.   *12 servings*

Prep time: 15 minutes
Cooking time: 20 minutes

MICROWAVE: • Place spinach and onions
in 2-quart casserole; cover. Microwave on
HIGH 3 to 4 minutes or until tender; drain.
• Beat cheeses and seasonings in small
mixing bowl at medium speed with electric
mixer until well blended. Stir in spinach
mixture; spread into 9-inch pie plate.
• Microwave on HIGH 4 to 6 minutes or
until thoroughly heated, stirring every
2 minutes. Stir before serving. Top with
remaining ingredients. Serve with crisp rye
crackers or bagel chips.

Microwave cooking time: 10 minutes

CHILLED PEAR HELENE SOUP

*Guests will be impressed with the elegant
presentation of this soup—and it's so
easy to prepare.*

4 pears, peeled, cored, cubed
1 (12 oz.) can pear nectar
1 (8 oz.) container Light
    PHILADELPHIA BRAND
    Pasteurized Process Cream Cheese
    Product
½ cup champagne
1 cup raspberries

- Place pears in food processor or blender
  container; process until smooth. Add
  nectar, cream cheese product and
  champagne; process until well blended.
  Pour into medium bowl; cover. Chill.
- When ready to serve, place raspberries in
  food processor or blender container;
  process until smooth. Strain.
- Spoon soup into individual serving bowls.
  Spoon approximately 2 tablespoons
  raspberry purée at intervals onto each
  serving. Pull wooden pick through purée
  making decorative design as desired.
  Garnish with additional raspberries and
  fresh mint leaves, if desired.

6 servings

Prep time: 10 minutes plus chilling

20

Chilled Pear Helene Soup

HERB ARTICHOKE SPREAD

1 (8 oz.) container PHILADELPHIA
   BRAND Soft Cream Cheese with
   Herb & Garlic
1 (6½ oz.) jar marinated artichoke
   hearts, drained, chopped
¼ teaspoon salt
4 to 6 drops hot pepper sauce

- Stir together ingredients in small bowl
  until well blended. Chill. Serve with
  toasted bread cutouts. Garnish with fresh
  herbs and chopped red pepper, if desired.
  1½ cups

Prep time: 5 minutes plus chilling

* * *

To make toasted bread cutouts, see directions page 18.

SEAFOOD RAVIOLI WITH FRESH TOMATO SAUCE

*PHILLY Soft Cream Cheese with Herb &
Garlic combined with imitation crabmeat
makes a tasty filling for these unique
ravioli appetizers.*

1 (8 oz.) container PHILADELPHIA
   BRAND Soft Cream Cheese with
   Herb & Garlic
¾ cup chopped LOUIS KEMP CRAB
   DELIGHTS Chunks, rinsed
36 wonton wrappers
   Cold water
   Fresh Tomato Sauce

- Stir together cream cheese and imitation
  crabmeat in medium bowl until well
  blended.
- For each ravioli, place 1 tablespoonful
  cream cheese mixture in center of one
  wonton wrapper. Brush edges with water.
  Place second wonton wrapper on top.
  Press edges together to seal, taking care to
  press out air. Repeat with remaining
  cream cheese mixture and wonton
  wrappers.
- For square-shaped ravioli, cut edges of
  wonton wrappers with pastry trimmer to
  form square. For round-shaped ravioli,
  place 3-inch round biscuit cutter on
  ravioli, making sure center of each cutter
  contains filling. Press down firmly, cutting
  through both wrappers, to trim edges.
  Repeat with remaining ravioli.
- Bring 1½ quarts water to boil in large
  saucepan. Cook ravioli, a few at a time,
  2 to 3 minutes or until they rise to
  surface. Remove with slotted spoon. Serve
  hot with Fresh Tomato Sauce.
  1½ dozen

FRESH TOMATO SAUCE

2 garlic cloves, minced
2 tablespoons olive oil
6 plum tomatoes, diced
1 tablespoon red wine vinegar
1 tablespoon chopped fresh parsley

- Sauté garlic in oil in medium saucepan
  1 minute. Add remaining ingredients.
- Cook over low heat 2 to 3 minutes or until
  thoroughly heated, stirring occasionally.
  Cool to room temperature.

Prep time: 25 minutes
Cooking time: 3 minutes per batch

Variation: For triangle-shaped ravioli, place
2 teaspoonfuls cream cheese mixture in
center of each wonton wrapper; brush
edges with water. Fold in half to form
triangle. Press edges together to seal, taking
care to press out air. Trim edges of wonton
wrapper with pastry trimmer, if desired.
3 dozen

Herb Artichoke Spread

ORIENTAL SPREAD

1 (12 oz.) container PHILADELPHIA
   BRAND Soft Cream Cheese
⅔ cup shredded carrots
½ cup chopped salted peanuts
¼ cup chopped water chestnuts
¼ cup green onion slices
2 tablespoons soy sauce
1 tablespoon chopped fresh cilantro
1 small garlic clove, minced
¼ teaspoon ground ginger
2 tablespoons sweet and sour sauce

- Spread cream cheese onto bottom of
  10-inch serving plate.
- Mix together all remaining ingredients
  except sweet and sour sauce in medium
  bowl. Spoon vegetable mixture evenly
  over cream cheese mixture to within
  ½ inch from edge. Drizzle with sauce.
  Serve with crackers.   *12 to 14 servings*

Prep time: 20 minutes

BACKYARD BRUNCH CITRUS DIP

*Add interest to these fruit kabob dippers
by cutting fruit into geometric shapes
before skewering.*

1 (8 oz.) pkg. Light PHILADELPHIA
   BRAND Neufchatel Cheese,
   softened
½ cup frozen orange juice concentrate,
   thawed
2 tablespoons skim milk

- Place ingredients in food processor or
  blender container; process until well
  blended. Chill. Serve with assorted fruit
  dippers.   *1½ cups*

Prep time: 5 minutes plus chilling

REGGAE DIP WITH SHRIMP

1 to 2 garlic cloves
1 (8 oz.) container PHILADELPHIA
   BRAND Soft Cream Cheese with
   Chives & Onion
¼ cup chili sauce
2 teaspoons worcestershire sauce
1 teaspoon dry mustard
¼ teaspoon pepper
30 medium shrimp, cleaned, cooked

- Place garlic in food processor or blender
  container; process until finely chopped.
- Add all remaining ingredients except
  shrimp; process until well blended. Chill.
  Serve with shrimp. Garnish with lemon
  wedges, if desired.   *6 servings*

Prep time: 15 minutes plus chilling

AVOCADO CRAB DIP

*PHILLY Neufchatel Cheese makes this dip
extra creamy.*

1 large avocado, halved, pitted, peeled
2 tablespoons chopped onion
1 tablespoon lemon juice
1 teaspoon worcestershire sauce
1 (8 oz.) pkg. Light PHILADELPHIA
   BRAND Neufchatel Cheese,
   softened
½ cup BREAKSTONE'S LIGHT
   CHOICE Sour Half and Half
½ teaspoon salt
   Few drops hot pepper sauce
1 (8 oz.) pkg. LOUIS KEMP CRAB
   DELIGHTS Legs, chopped

- Place avocado, onion, lemon juice and
  worcestershire sauce in food processor or
  blender container; process until blended.
- Add neufchatel cheese, sour half and half,
  salt and hot pepper sauce; process until
  well blended. Stir in imitation crab meat.
  Serve with tortilla chips.   *3 cups*

Prep time: 10 minutes

24

SPINACH BALLS

2 (10 oz.) pkgs. BIRDS EYE Chopped
    Spinach, thawed, well drained
1 (8 oz.) container PHILADELPHIA
    BRAND Soft Cream Cheese with
    Herb & Garlic
2 eggs
⅔ cup (3 ozs.) KRAFT 100% Grated
    Parmesan Cheese
½ cup dry bread crumbs

- Preheat oven to 375°.
- Stir together all ingredients in large bowl
  until well blended. Shape into 1-inch balls.
  Place in 15×10×1-inch jelly roll pan.
- Bake 15 to 20 minutes or until firm. Serve
  with heated spaghetti sauce, if desired.
  Approximately 3½ dozen

Prep time: 20 minutes
Cooking time: 20 minutes

---

*For well-drained spinach, layer thawed
spinach between paper towels and firmly
squeeze out all excess moisture; repeat as
necessary with additional paper towels.*

HOT AND SPICY CHICKEN NUGGETS

*This creamy salsa dip is a natural
accompaniment for popular chicken
nuggets.*

1 (8 oz.) container PHILADELPHIA
    BRAND Soft Cream Cheese
½ cup salsa
2 tablespoons milk
½ teaspoon ground cumin
½ teaspoon onion powder
½ teaspoon garlic powder
¼ to ½ teaspoon cayenne pepper
2 (10.5 oz.) pkgs. frozen chicken
    nuggets

- Stir together all ingredients except
  chicken nuggets in small bowl until well
  blended. Chill.
- Prepare chicken nuggets according to
  package directions. Serve with cream
  cheese dip.　　*Approximately 3 dozen*

Prep time: 10 minutes plus chilling
Cooking time: Approximately 20 minutes

ROASTED GARLIC DIP

2 heads (4 ozs.) garlic
1 (8 oz.) pkg. PHILADELPHIA
    BRAND Cream Cheese, softened
¼ cup chopped roasted red peppers
2 tablespoons dry Marsala wine
2 tablespoons olive oil
¼ teaspoon salt
⅛ teaspoon white pepper

- Preheat oven to 350°.
- Remove outer papery skin from both
  heads of garlic, leaving heads intact; place
  in small baking dish. Add water to dish to
  1-inch depth; cover with foil.
- Bake 1 hour or until garlic is tender,
  basting occasionally with water.
- Remove skins from garlic cloves; place
  garlic in food processor or blender
  container. Add remaining ingredients;
  process until smooth. Chill. Garnish with
  chopped fresh chives and red pepper, if
  desired. Serve with vegetable dippers.
  1½ cups

Prep time: 10 minutes plus chilling
Cooking time: 1 hour

From Breakfast-to-Dessert Breads

BREAKFAST RAISIN RING

PHILLY Cream Cheese adds a delicate flavor and texture to this coffeecake and filling.

> 1 (8 oz.) pkg. PHILADELPHIA
>   BRAND Cream Cheese, cubed
> 1 cup cold water
> 1 (16 oz.) pkg. hot roll mix
> 1 egg
> 1 teaspoon vanilla
> ½ cup packed brown sugar
> ⅓ cup PARKAY Margarine
> ¼ cup granulated sugar
> 1½ teaspoons ground cinnamon
> 1½ teaspoons vanilla
> ½ cup golden raisins
>   Vanilla Drizzle

- Preheat oven to 350°.
- Blend 6 ounces cream cheese and water in small saucepan. Cook over low heat until mixture reaches 115° to 120°, stirring occasionally.
- Stir together hot roll mix and yeast packet in large bowl. Add cream cheese mixture, egg and 1 teaspoon vanilla, mixing until dough pulls away from sides of bowl.
- Knead dough on lightly floured surface 5 minutes or until smooth and elastic. Cover; let rise in warm place 20 minutes.
- Beat remaining cream cheese, brown sugar, margarine, granulated sugar, cinnamon and 1½ teaspoons vanilla in small mixing bowl at medium speed with electric mixer until well blended.
- Roll out dough to 20×12-inch rectangle; spread cream cheese mixture over dough to within 1½ inches from outer edges of dough. Sprinkle with raisins.
- Roll up from long end, sealing edges. Place, seam side down, on greased cookie sheet; shape into ring, pressing ends together to seal. Make 1-inch cuts through ring from outer edge at 2-inch intervals. Cover; let rise in warm place 30 minutes.
- Bake 30 to 40 minutes or until golden brown. Cool slightly. Drizzle with Vanilla Drizzle.   *8 to 10 servings*

VANILLA DRIZZLE

> 1 cup powdered sugar
> 1 to 2 tablespoons milk
> 1 teaspoon vanilla
> ½ teaspoon ground cinnamon
>   (optional)

- Stir ingredients together in small bowl until smooth.

Prep time: 30 minutes plus rising
Cooking time: 40 minutes

To knead dough, place on lightly floured surface. With floured hands, fold dough toward you with fingers; push firmly away with heel of hand. Give dough a quarter turn; repeat. Add additional flour to surface as needed to prevent sticking.

26

Breakfast Raisin Ring

HOME–STYLE BLUEBERRY MUFFINS

PHILLY Cream Cheese makes these much more than "just muffins."

> 1 (8 oz.) pkg. PHILADELPHIA
>   BRAND Cream Cheese, softened
> ¼ cup sugar
> 1 egg yolk
> 1 teaspoon vanilla
> 1 (23.5 oz.) pkg. bakery-style
>   blueberry muffin mix
> ¾ cup cold water
> 1 egg
> 1 teaspoon grated lemon peel
> 1 teaspoon ground cinnamon

- Preheat oven to 400°.
- Beat cream cheese, sugar, egg yolk and vanilla in small mixing bowl at medium speed with electric mixer until well blended.
- Rinse and drain blueberries from muffin mix. Stir together muffin mix, water, egg and peel in large bowl (mixture will be lumpy). Stir in blueberries. Pour into well-greased medium-size muffin pan.
- Spoon cream cheese mixture over batter; sprinkle with combined topping mix and cinnamon.
- Bake 18 to 22 minutes or until lightly browned. Cool 5 minutes. Loosen muffins from rim of pan; cool before removing from pan.   *1 dozen*

Prep time: 20 minutes
Cooking time: 22 minutes

Tough muffins full of holes are the result of overmixing. For tender muffins, make a well in the combined dry ingredients. Pour combined liquids, all at once, into the well. Stir just enough to moisten dry ingredients. Do not overmix.

CARAMEL–PECAN STICKY BUNS

PHILLY Cream Cheese adds its special flavor to the dough.

> 1 (8 oz.) pkg. PHILADELPHIA
>   BRAND Cream Cheese, cubed
> ¾ cup cold water
> 1 (16 oz.) pkg. hot roll mix
> 1 egg
> ⅓ cup granulated sugar
> 1 teaspoon ground cinnamon
> 1 cup pecan halves
> ¾ cup packed brown sugar
> ½ cup light corn syrup
> ¼ cup PARKAY Margarine, melted

- Preheat oven to 350°.
- Stir together 6 ounces cream cheese and water in small saucepan. Cook over low heat until mixture reaches 115° to 120°, stirring occasionally.
- Stir together hot roll mix and yeast packet in large bowl. Add cream cheese mixture and egg, mixing until dough pulls away from sides of bowl.
- Knead dough on lightly floured surface 5 minutes or until smooth and elastic. Cover; let rise in warm place 20 minutes.
- Beat remaining cream cheese, granulated sugar and cinnamon in small mixing bowl at medium speed with electric mixer until well blended.
- Roll out dough to 18×12-inch rectangle; spread cream cheese mixture over dough to within 1 inch from outer edges of dough.
- Roll up from long end, sealing edges. Cut into twenty-four ¾-inch slices.
- Stir together remaining ingredients in small bowl. Spoon 2 teaspoonfuls pecan mixture into bottoms of greased medium-sized muffin pans.
- Place dough, cut side up, in cups. Cover; let rise in warm place 30 minutes.
- Bake 20 to 25 minutes or until golden brown. Invert onto serving platter immediately.   *2 dozen*

Prep time: 30 minutes plus rising
Cooking time: 25 minutes

28

Top to bottom: Home-Style Blueberry Muffins;
Caramel-Pecan Sticky Buns

CHERRY CREAM CHEESE COFFEECAKE

Serve this delicious coffeecake warm with your favorite GENERAL FOODS International Coffee.

1½ cups flour
1 cup old-fashioned or quick oats, uncooked
¾ cup sugar
¾ cup PARKAY Margarine
½ cup BREAKSTONE'S Sour Cream
1 egg
½ teaspoon baking soda
1 (8 oz.) pkg. PHILADELPHIA BRAND Cream Cheese, softened
¼ cup sugar
¼ teaspoon almond extract
1 egg
¾ cup cherry pie filling
⅓ cup sliced almonds

- Preheat oven to 350°.
- Mix together flour, oats and ¾ cup sugar in large bowl; cut in margarine until mixture resembles coarse crumbs. Reserve 1 cup crumb mixture.
- Add sour cream, one egg and soda to remaining crumb mixture; mix well. Spread onto bottom and 2 inches up sides of greased 9-inch springform pan.
- Beat cream cheese, ¼ cup sugar and extract in small mixing bowl at medium speed with electric mixer until well blended. Blend in one egg. Pour into crust.
- Top with pie filling. Sprinkle with reserved crumb mixture and almonds.
- Bake 50 to 55 minutes or until golden brown. Cool 15 minutes. Carefully remove rim of pan. Serve warm or at room temperature.   *10 servings*

Prep time: 20 minutes
Cooking time: 55 minutes

Variation: Substitute KRAFT Red Raspberry Preserves for pie filling.

CREAM CHEESE AND PECAN DANISH

1 sheet frozen ready-to-bake puff pastry, thawed
2 (3 oz.) pkgs. PHILADELPHIA BRAND Cream Cheese, softened
¼ cup powdered sugar
1 egg
1 teaspoon vanilla
¾ cup chopped pecans
Creamy Glaze

- Preheat oven to 375°.
- Unfold pastry; roll to 15×10-inch rectangle. Place in 15×10×1-inch jelly roll pan.
- Beat 6 ounces cream cheese, ¼ cup sugar, egg and vanilla in small mixing bowl at medium speed with electric mixer until well blended. Stir in ½ cup pecans.
- Spread cream cheese mixture over pastry to within 3 inches from outer edges.
- Make 2-inch cuts at 1-inch intervals on long sides of pastry. Crisscross strips over filling.
- Bake 25 to 30 minutes or until golden brown. Cool.
- Drizzle with Creamy Glaze. Sprinkle with remaining pecans.   *10 to 12 servings*

CREAMY GLAZE

1 (3 oz.) pkg. PHILADELPHIA BRAND Cream Cheese, softened
¾ cup powdered sugar
1 tablespoon milk

- Beat ingredients until smooth.

Prep time: 20 minutes
Cooking time: 30 minutes

30

31

Cream Cheese and Pecan Danish

ORANGE DANISH COFFEECAKE

This easy coffeecake is a sure sensation for any gathering.

    2 cups variety baking mix
    ¾ cup orange juice
    ½ cup granulated sugar
    1 egg
    1 (8 oz.) pkg. PHILADELPHIA
        BRAND Cream Cheese, softened
    ¼ cup granulated sugar
    1 egg
    1 teaspoon vanilla
    ⅓ cup packed brown sugar
    ⅓ cup chopped nuts
    1 teaspoon grated orange peel
    ½ teaspoon ground cinnamon

- Preheat oven to 350°.
- Stir together baking mix, orange juice, ½ cup granulated sugar and one egg in medium bowl; pour into greased 9-inch square baking pan. Bake 10 minutes.
- Beat cream cheese, ¼ cup granulated sugar, one egg and vanilla in small mixing bowl at medium speed with electric mixer until well blended; pour over cake.
- Top with combined remaining ingredients.
- Bake 20 minutes.   *6 to 8 servings*

Prep time: 20 minutes
Cooking time: 20 minutes

EASTER BUNS WITH VANILLA GLAZE

A special Easter treat... PHILLY Soft Cream Cheese with Pineapple and piña colada yogurt add the unique rich flavor and texture to these delicious rolls.

    1 (8 oz.) container PHILADELPHIA
        BRAND Soft Cream Cheese with
        Pineapple
    1 (8 oz.) container piña colada-
        flavored yogurt
    2 tablespoons PARKAY Margarine
    1 (16 oz.) pkg. hot roll mix
    ⅓ cup granulated sugar
    1 egg
    Vanilla Glaze

- Preheat oven to 350°.
- Stir together cream cheese, yogurt and margarine in small saucepan until well blended. Cook over low heat until mixture reaches 115° to 120°, stirring occasionally.
- Stir together hot roll mix, yeast packet and granulated sugar in large bowl. Add cream cheese mixture and egg, mixing until dough pulls away from sides of bowl.
- Knead dough on lightly floured surface 5 minutes or until smooth and elastic. Cover; let rise in warm place 20 minutes.
- Divide dough into twenty four balls. Place 2 inches apart on greased cookie sheets. Cut crisscross design with knife on top of balls, ½ inch deep. Cover; let rise in warm place 30 minutes.
- Bake 20 to 22 minutes or until lightly browned. Dip warm buns into Vanilla Glaze.   *2 dozen*

VANILLA GLAZE

    1½ cups powdered sugar
    3 tablespoons light corn syrup
    3 tablespoons cold water
    2 teaspoons vanilla

- Stir together ingredients in small bowl until smooth.

Prep time: 30 minutes plus rising
Cooking time: 22 minutes

32

33

Easter Buns with Vanilla Glase

LEMON CRANBERRY LOAF

1 (8 oz.) pkg. PHILADELPHIA
    BRAND Cream Cheese, softened
⅓ cup PARKAY Margarine
1¼ cups sugar
1 teaspoon vanilla
3 eggs
2 tablespoons lemon juice
1 teaspoon grated lemon peel
1½ cups chopped cranberries
2¼ cups flour
2 teaspoons CALUMET Baking Powder
½ teaspoon baking soda

- Preheat oven to 325°.
- Beat cream cheese, margarine, sugar and vanilla in large mixing bowl at medium speed with electric mixer until well blended. Add eggs, one at a time, mixing well after each addition. Stir in lemon juice and peel.
- Toss together cranberries with combined dry ingredients in large bowl. Add cream cheese mixture, mixing just until moistened.
- Pour into greased and floured 9×5-inch loaf pan. Bake 1 hour and 15 minutes. Cool 5 minutes; remove from pan. Cool completely.   *1 loaf*

Prep time: 15 minutes
Cooking time: 1 hour and 15 minutes

PEAR CREAM BREAKFAST CAKE

Incredibly delicious ... perfect for brunch or as a delicious dessert.

1 (29 oz.) can pear halves in heavy
    syrup, undrained
1 (8 oz.) pkg. PHILADELPHIA
    BRAND Cream Cheese, softened
¼ cup KRAFT Apricot Preserves
2 tablespoons PARKAY Margarine
1 (9 oz.) pkg. yellow cake mix
2 tablespoons oil
1 egg
1 teaspoon ground ginger

- Preheat oven to 350°.
- Drain pears, reserving ½ cup syrup. Slice pears; place on bottom of 8-inch square baking pan.
- Beat cream cheese, preserves and margarine in small mixing bowl at medium speed with electric mixer until well blended; pour over pears.
- Beat cake mix, reserved syrup, oil, egg and ginger in large mixing bowl at medium speed with electric mixer until well blended; pour over cream cheese mixture.
- Bake 35 to 40 minutes or until golden brown. Serve warm with half and half.
                    8 to 10 servings

Prep time: 15 minutes
Cooking time: 40 minutes

34

Pear Cream Breakfast Cake

FRENCH CUSTARD MORNING SQUARES

2 (8 oz.) pkgs. PHILADELPHIA
    BRAND Cream Cheese, softened
½ cup granulated sugar
1 teaspoon vanilla
1 egg, separated
2 (8 oz.) cans refrigerated quick
    crescent dinner rolls
Sifted powdered sugar

- Preheat oven to 350°.
- Beat cream cheese, granulated sugar, vanilla and egg yolk in large mixing bowl at medium speed with electric mixer until well blended.
- Place half of dough in 13×9-inch baking pan; press perforations together to seal. Bake 10 minutes.
- Pour cream cheese mixture over crust. Place remaining dough on waxed paper; roll to 13×9-inch rectangle. Invert dough onto cream cheese mixture; remove waxed paper. Brush top with beaten egg white.
- Bake 20 to 25 minutes or until golden brown. Cool. Sprinkle with powdered sugar.   *12 to 15 servings*

Prep time: 20 minutes
Cooking time: 25 minutes

CARDAMOM BRAID

1 (8 oz.) pkg. PHILADELPHIA
    BRAND Cream Cheese, cubed
⅔ cup cold water
1 (16 oz.) pkg. hot roll mix
⅓ cup sugar
1 teaspoon ground cardamom
1 egg, beaten
1 to 2 tablespoons milk
1 tablespoon sugar

- Place cream cheese and water in small saucepan. Cook over low heat until mixture reaches 115° to 120°, stirring occasionally until smooth. Remove from heat.
- Stir together hot roll mix, yeast packet, ⅓ cup sugar and cardamom in large bowl. Add cream cheese mixture and egg, mixing until dough pulls away from sides of bowl.
- On floured surface, knead dough 5 minutes or until smooth and elastic. Cover; let rest in warm place 20 minutes.
- Divide dough into thirds. Roll each third into 16-inch rope; braid, pinching ends together to seal. Place braid on greased cookie sheet.
- Cover; let rise in warm place 30 minutes. Brush with milk; sprinkle with 1 tablespoon sugar.
- Preheat oven to 375°.
- Bake 25 to 30 minutes or until light golden brown. Serve with PHILADELPHIA BRAND Soft Cream Cheese and KRAFT Apricot Preserves, if desired.   *1 loaf*

Prep time: 20 minutes plus rising
Cooking time: 30 minutes

Variation: Add one (6 oz.) package diced mixed dried fruit to dry ingredients.

Cardamom, a member of the ginger family, is an aromatic, sweet spice. Popular in India and Scandinavian countries, it is used in much the same way we use cinnamon-sugar blends.

36

BANANA–SCOTCH BREAKFAST CAKE

1 (8 oz.) pkg. PHILADELPHIA
   BRAND Cream Cheese, softened
⅓ cup oil
2 eggs
½ teaspoon vanilla
½ cup cold water
1 (14 oz.) pkg. banana bread mix
½ cup chopped pecans, toasted
½ cup currants
1½ cups butterscotch morsels
   Powdered sugar

- Preheat oven to 350°.
- Beat cream cheese, oil, eggs and vanilla in large mixing bowl at medium speed with electric mixer until well blended. Gradually blend in water.
- Stir in bread mix, mixing just until moistened. Stir in pecans and currants. Pour into greased and floured 13×9-inch baking pan.
- Sprinkle with butterscotch morsels; gently press into batter.
- Bake 35 minutes or until wooden pick inserted in center comes out clean. Cool. Sprinkle lightly with powdered sugar just before serving. *12 servings*

Prep time: 20 minutes
Cooking time: 35 minutes

PIÑA COLADA COFFEECAKE

¼ cup chopped almonds
¼ cup packed brown sugar
¼ cup BAKER'S ANGEL FLAKE
   Coconut
2 tablespoons flour
1 teaspoon ground cinnamon
1 (10 oz.) container frozen piña colada
   fruit mixer concentrate, thawed
1 (8 oz.) pkg. PHILADELPHIA
   BRAND Cream Cheese, softened
2 tablespoons lime juice
3 eggs
1 (18.25 oz.) pkg. white cake mix
   Lime Glaze

- Preheat oven to 350°.
- Stir together almonds, brown sugar, coconut, flour and cinnamon in small bowl.
- Reserve 3 tablespoons piña colada concentrate for use in Lime Glaze. Beat cream cheese, remaining concentrate and 2 tablespoons lime juice in large mixing bowl at medium speed with electric mixer until well blended.
- Add eggs, one at a time, mixing well after each addition. Add cake mix; beat until well blended.
- Pour half of batter into greased and floured 10-inch fluted tube pan. Sprinkle almond mixture over batter; top with remaining batter.
- Bake 55 to 60 minutes or until wooden pick inserted in center comes out clean. Cool. Drizzle with Lime Glaze.
  10 to 12 servings

LIME GLAZE

3 tablespoons reserved piña colada
   concentrate
2 teaspoons lime juice
1½ cups sifted powdered sugar

- Stir together reserved concentrate and 2 teaspoons lime juice in small bowl until smooth; gradually stir in powdered sugar.

Prep time: 25 minutes
Cooking time: 1 hour

Simple & Elegant Entertaining

GRILLED LAMB SHASHLYK WITH MINTED CREAM SAUCE

PHILLY Cream Cheese, yogurt and mint are a perfect blend of flavors to complement these grilled lamb kabobs.

    2 lbs. lean lamb, cut into 1½-inch cubes
    ½ cup SEVEN SEAS VIVA Red Wine!
        Vinegar & Oil Reduced Calorie
        Dressing
    1 green pepper, cut into 1-inch chunks
    1 red pepper, cut into 1-inch chunks
    1 yellow pepper, cut into 1-inch chunks
    1 small red onion, cut into wedges
    1 lemon, thinly sliced
        Minted Cream Sauce

- Marinate lamb in dressing in refrigerator several hours or overnight. Drain, reserving marinade for basting.
- Prepare coals for grilling.
- Arrange lamb, vegetables and lemon on skewers. Place on greased grill over hot coals (coals will be glowing).
- Grill, uncovered, 4 to 6 minutes on each side or to desired doneness, brushing frequently with reserved marinade. Serve with Minted Cream Sauce.   *8 servings*

MINTED CREAM SAUCE

    1 (8 oz.) container PHILADELPHIA
        BRAND Soft Cream Cheese
    ½ cup plain yogurt
    2 tablespoons chopped fresh mint
    1 garlic clove, minced
    ⅛ teaspoon black pepper

- Place ingredients in food processor or blender container; process until well blended.

Prep time: 20 minutes plus marinating
Cooking time: 12 minutes

CHICKEN RAGOUT WITH ORZO

    ⅔ cup chopped onion
    1 (4 oz.) can mushrooms, drained
    ⅓ cup celery slices
    ⅓ cup finely chopped carrot
    ¼ lb. Italian sausage, casing removed, crumbled
    4 OSCAR MAYER Bacon Slices, chopped
    1 tablespoon olive oil
    1½ lbs. boneless skinless chicken breasts, cut into ½-inch pieces
    1 bay leaf
    1 large garlic clove, minced
    ¾ cup dry Marsala wine
    1 (14½ oz.) can tomatoes, cut up, undrained
    1 cup chicken broth
    ⅛ teaspoon ground cloves
    1 (8 oz.) container PHILADELPHIA
        BRAND Soft Cream Cheese with
        Olives & Pimento
    ¾ cup (4 ozs.) orzo, cooked, drained

- Sauté onions, mushrooms, celery, carrots, sausage and bacon in oil in Dutch oven 5 minutes.
- Add chicken, bay leaf and garlic; cook, stirring occasionally, 4 minutes.
- Add wine. Bring to boil; reduce heat to medium. Simmer 10 to 15 minutes or until only slight amount of liquid remains.
- Stir in tomatoes, broth and cloves. Bring to boil over medium-high heat; reduce heat to medium. Simmer 20 minutes or until slightly thickened. Remove from heat.
- Stir in cream cheese and orzo; mix well.
                                    6 servings

Prep time: 30 minutes
Cooking time: 40 minutes

39

Grilled Lamb Shashlyk with Minted Cream Sauce

SIMPLE & ELEGANT ENTERTAINING

BEEF TENDERLOIN EN CROUTE

You'll receive rave reviews when you serve this elegant entrée.

   1 (3 to 4 lb.) beef tenderloin
   ½ lb. mushrooms, finely chopped
   2 tablespoons PARKAY Margarine
   1 (8 oz.) container PHILADELPHIA
       BRAND Soft Cream Cheese with
       Herb & Garlic
   ¼ cup seasoned dry bread crumbs
   2 tablespoons Madeira wine
   1 tablespoon chopped fresh chives
   ¼ teaspoon salt
   1 (17¼ oz.) pkg. frozen ready-to-bake
       puff pastry sheets
   1 egg, beaten
   1 tablespoon cold water

- Preheat oven to 425°.
- Tie meat with string at 1-inch intervals, if necessary. Place meat on rack in baking pan.
- Roast 45 to 50 minutes or until meat thermometer registers 135°. Remove from oven; cool 30 minutes in refrigerator. Remove string.
- Sauté mushrooms in margarine in large skillet 10 minutes or until liquid evaporates, stirring occasionally.
- Add cream cheese, bread crumbs, wine, chives and salt; mix well. Cool.
- Thaw puff pastry sheets according to package directions.
- On lightly floured surface, overlap pastry sheets ½ inch to form 14×12-inch rectangle; press edges firmly together to seal. Trim length of pastry 2½ inches longer than length of meat.
- Place meat in center of pastry; spread mushroom mixture over top and sides of meat.

- Fold pastry over meat; press edges together to seal. Decorate top with pastry trimmings, if desired.
- Brush pastry with combined egg and water. Place meat in greased 15×10×1-inch jelly roll pan.
- Bake 20 to 25 minutes or until pastry is golden brown. Let stand 10 minutes before slicing to serve.   *8 to 10 servings*

Prep time: 1 hour plus chilling
Cooking time: 25 minutes

━━━━━━━━━━━━━ ◆◆◆ ━━━━━━━━━━━━━

The simplest and most accurate way to check for doneness in meat is to use a meat thermometer. The thermometer should be inserted into the thickest part of the meat, making sure not to touch any bone. It will register 140° for rare meat, 160° for medium. The temperature of the meat will rise 5° to 10° during standing, so for perfect doneness remove meat from the oven accordingly.

40

Beef Tenderloin en Croute

LAKESIDE LOBSTER TAILS

PHILLY Cream Cheese blended with white wine and onions makes a simple but splendid topping for fresh lobster tails.

> 4 (1 lb. each) cleaned lobster tails with shells
> Herb Wine Sauce

- Prepare coals for grilling.
- Cut each lobster tail through center of back with knife or kitchen shears; split open.
- Place lobster, shell side down, on greased grill over hot coals (coals will be glowing). Grill, covered, 5 to 8 minutes on each side or until shell is bright red and lobster meat is white.
- Serve with Herb Wine Sauce. Garnish with lemon wedges, if desired.

4 servings

HERB WINE SAUCE

> 1 (8 oz.) container PHILADELPHIA BRAND Soft Cream Cheese with Herb & Garlic
> ¼ cup dry white wine
> 2 green onions, thinly sliced
> ½ teaspoon salt

- Stir together ingredients in small bowl until well blended.

Prep time: 15 minutes
Cooking time: 16 minutes

BARBECUED SALSA TENDERLOIN

Pickled jalapeño peppers are available in most grocery stores. If unavailable, substitute a fresh jalapeño pepper.

> 3 (2 to 2½ lbs. total) pork tenderloins
> 1 (14½ oz.) can whole peeled tomatoes, undrained, coarsely chopped
> 1 small onion, chopped
> 3 green onions, thinly sliced
> 1 pickled jalapeño pepper, minced
> ¼ cup chopped fresh Italian parsley
> ¼ cup oil
> 2 tablespoons lime juice
> 1 garlic clove, minced
> ½ teaspoon black pepper
> ¼ teaspoon salt
> 1 (8 oz.) pkg. Light PHILADELPHIA BRAND Neufchatel Cheese, cubed

- Prepare coals for grilling.
- Marinate meat in combined remaining ingredients, except for neufchatel cheese, in refrigerator 30 minutes, turning meat occasionally. Drain, reserving marinade for sauce.
- Place meat on greased grill over medium coals (coals will have slight glow). Grill, covered, 45 to 55 minutes or until internal temperature reaches 170°, turning occasionally.
- Bring reserved marinade to boil in small saucepan; reduce heat to low. Add neufchatel cheese; stir until melted. Serve over meat.

8 servings

Prep time: 30 minutes plus marinating
Cooking time: 55 minutes

For a distinct smoky flavor, add hardwood chips to the white-hot charcoal fire. The varieties of hardwood chips available include cherry, hickory, apple, oak, pecan and mesquite. Of the varieties mentioned, mesquite produces the most intense smoky flavor. Never use softwoods, such as pine; softwoods impart an objectionable resinous flavor.

43

Lakeside Lobster Tails

GRILLED SALMON WITH CREAMY CUCUMBER SAUCE

    6 to 8 salmon fillets, 1 to 1½ inches
        thick
    ¼ cup olive oil
    2 tablespoons chopped fresh dill or
        1 teaspoon dried dill weed
    1 tablespoon lime juice
        Creamy Cucumber Sauce

• Marinate salmon in combined oil, dill and
  lime juice in refrigerator at least 1 hour.
  Drain.
• Prepare coals for grilling.
• Place salmon on greased grill over hot
  coals (coals will be glowing). Grill,
  covered, 5 to 8 minutes on each side or
  until fish flakes easily with fork. Serve
  with Creamy Cucumber Sauce. Garnish
  with fresh dill sprig, if desired.

8 servings

CREAMY CUCUMBER SAUCE

    1 (8 oz.) pkg. Light PHILADELPHIA
        BRAND Neufchatel Cheese,
        softened
    3 tablespoons lime juice
    3 tablespoons skim milk
    2 tablespoons chopped fresh dill or
        1 teaspoon dried dill weed
    ¼ teaspoon salt
    ⅛ teaspoon pepper
    1 cucumber, peeled, seeded, chopped

• Beat all ingredients except cucumber in
  small mixing bowl at medium speed with
  electric mixer until well blended. Stir in
  cucumber.

Prep time: 30 minutes plus marinating
Cooking time: 16 minutes

Note: For thinner sauce, increase skim milk
by 1 to 2 tablespoons.

◆ ◆ ◆

*Salmon and swordfish steaks are excel-
lent types of fish for grilling because of
their firm flesh. Lightly brush the surface
of the fish and grill grate with vegetable
oil to prevent sticking.*

CORNBREAD–STUFFED TURKEY BREAST

*PHILLY Soft Cream Cheese with
Pineapple adds a hint of sweetness to this
savory stuffing.*

    1 (3½ to 4 lb.) LOUIS RICH Fresh
        Turkey Breast Half
    1 (8 oz.) container PHILADELPHIA
        BRAND Soft Cream Cheese with
        Pineapple
    2 cups crumbled cornbread
    1 egg, beaten
    ½ cup chopped onion
    ¼ cup chopped pecans, toasted
    1½ teaspoons poultry seasoning

• Preheat oven to 325°.
• Rinse turkey; pat dry. Loosen skin with
  knife; pull back skin, leaving skin attached
  along one edge.
• Stir together remaining ingredients in
  medium bowl until well blended. Place
  mixture between meat and skin. Replace
  skin; secure with wooden picks. Place in
  roasting pan.
• Bake 1 hour to 1 hour and 30 minutes or
  until meat thermometer registers 160°,
  brushing occasionally with pan drippings.
  Let stand, covered, 15 minutes before
  slicing. Remove wooden picks.

8 servings

Prep time: 15 minutes plus standing
Cooking time: 1 hour and 30 minutes

44

Grilled Salmon with Creamy Cucumber Sauce

PASTA TOSSED WITH BLUE CHEESE SAUCE

A quick, yet elegant recipe using leftover ham.

   1 cup coarsely chopped leeks
   ¼ cup coarsely chopped pecans
   2 tablespoons PARKAY Margarine
1½ cups ham strips
   ¼ cup Madeira wine or chicken broth
   1 garlic clove, minced
   1 (8 oz.) container PHILADELPHIA
      BRAND Soft Cream Cheese
   2 tablespoons milk
   ½ cup (2 ozs.) KRAFT Blue Cheese
      Crumbles
   8 ozs. fettuccine, cooked, drained

• Sauté leeks and pecans in margarine in medium skillet until leeks are tender. Add ham; cook until thoroughly heated.
• Cook wine and garlic in medium saucepan over low heat 1 minute. Add cream cheese and milk; stir until cream cheese is smooth. Remove from heat; stir in blue cheese.
• Toss all ingredients together. Serve immediately.   *4 servings*

Prep time: 15 minutes
Cooking time: 15 minutes

Variation: Substitute OSCAR MAYER Smoked Cooked Ham Slices, cut into strips, for ham strips.

MICROWAVE: • Place leeks, pecans and margarine in 1-quart casserole; cover.
• Microwave on HIGH 3 to 5 minutes or until leeks are tender, stirring after 2 minutes. Stir in ham. • Microwave on HIGH 2 to 3 minutes or until thoroughly heated. • Microwave wine and garlic in 1-quart bowl on HIGH 1 to 2 minutes or until hot. Stir in cream cheese and milk.
• Microwave on HIGH 2 to 3 minutes or until cream cheese is smooth, stirring every minute. Stir in blue cheese. Toss all ingredients together. Serve immediately.

Microwave cooking time: 13 minutes

46

Leeks are a member of the onion family. Look for leeks that are 1 to 1½ inches in diameter. The base and white section of the leaves are the edible parts of the leek. Trim off root ends and all but 2 inches of the green tops before chopping. Wash carefully to remove sand.

SWORDFISH WITH LEEK CREAM

Serve this entrée with fresh green beans and a tossed salad for a special dinner made easy.

   4 (1 to 1½ lbs. total) swordfish steaks
   2 tablespoons olive oil
      Leek Cream

• Prepare coals for grilling.
• Brush fish with oil.
• Place fish on greased grill over hot coals (coals will be glowing). Grill, uncovered, 3 to 4 minutes on each side or until fish flakes easily with fork. Serve with Leek Cream.   *4 servings*

LEEK CREAM
   1 leek, cut into 1-inch strips
   2 tablespoons PARKAY Margarine
   1 (3 oz.) pkg. PHILADELPHIA
      BRAND Cream Cheese, cubed
   3 tablespoons dry white wine
   2 tablespoons chopped fresh parsley
   ½ teaspoon garlic salt
   ¼ teaspoon pepper

• Sauté leeks in margarine in medium skillet until tender. Add remaining ingredients; stir over low heat until cream cheese is melted.

Prep time: 15 minutes
Cooking time: 8 minutes

47

HERB–CRUSTED PORK ROAST WITH APRICOT FILLING

This savory roast, seasoned with a variety of herbs, is made extra special with a creamy apricot filling.

  1 (3½ to 4 lb.) center-cut boneless pork roast
  1 (8 oz.) container PHILADELPHIA BRAND Soft Cream Cheese with Chives & Onion
  1 cup chopped dried apricots
  1 garlic clove, minced
  2 teaspoons dried rosemary leaves, crushed
  1 teaspoon dried thyme leaves, crushed
  ¾ teaspoon pepper
  ½ teaspoon salt
  1 tablespoon oil
    Gravy

- Preheat oven to 325°.
- Remove string from meat. Cut 2½-inch wide pocket through meat.
- Stir together cream cheese and apricots in small bowl until well blended; fill meat pocket with apricot mixture.
- Coat meat with combined garlic and seasonings; pat with oil. Place meat, fat side up, on rack in baking pan.
- Roast 1 hour to 1 hour and 30 minutes or until meat thermometer registers 165°. Let stand, covered, 10 to 15 minutes before slicing. (Temperature will rise 5° to 10° during standing.) Remove meat to platter, reserving ¼ cup pan drippings for Gravy. Keep meat warm. Serve with Gravy.   *10 to 12 servings*

GRAVY

  ¼ cup reserved pan drippings
  3 tablespoons flour
    Cold water
  ¼ teaspoon salt
  ⅛ teaspoon pepper

- Pour drippings into small saucepan. Stir in flour. Cook over low heat, stirring constantly, until mixture comes to boil.
- Gradually stir in 1 cup water; cook, stirring constantly, until mixture boils and thickens.
- Add additional water, 1 tablespoon at a time, if necessary, to reach desired consistency. Stir in salt and pepper.

Prep time: 25 minutes plus standing
Cooking time: 1 hour and 30 minutes

◆ ◆ ◆

A cooked mixture of fat and flour whisked together, otherwise known as roux, is the thickening element in many gravies and sauces. In this recipe, the fat comes from the pan drippings, giving the gravy a rich, delicious flavor. It is important to cook the roux slowly and evenly, whisking constantly, so as not to impart a burnt flavor to the gravy.

48

Herb-Crusted Pork Roast with Apricot Filling

SENSATIONAL SPINACH PIE

1 lb. Italian sausage, casing removed, cooked, crumbled
1 (15 oz.) container ricotta cheese
1 (10 oz.) pkg. BIRDS EYE Chopped Spinach, thawed, well drained
1 (8 oz.) container PHILADELPHIA BRAND Soft Cream Cheese with Herb & Garlic
1 cup (4 ozs.) KRAFT Shredded Low-Moisture Part-Skim Mozzarella Cheese
2 eggs, beaten
½ teaspoon hot pepper sauce
1 (15 oz.) pkg. refrigerated pie crusts (2 crusts)
1 egg, beaten

- Preheat oven to 400°.
- Mix together sausage, ricotta cheese, spinach, cream cheese, mozzarella cheese, two eggs and hot pepper sauce in large bowl until well blended.
- On lightly floured surface, roll out one pie crust to 12-inch circle.
- Place in 10-inch pie plate; fill with sausage mixture.
- Roll remaining pie crust to 12-inch circle; make decorative cutouts in pastry, if desired. Place pastry over filling. Seal and flute edges of pie. Decorate top with additional pastry; cut into decorative shapes, if desired. Brush with remaining egg.
- Bake 35 to 40 minutes or until pastry is light golden brown. Serve warm or at room temperature.   *10 servings*

Prep time: 20 minutes
Cooking time: 40 minutes

GRILLED TURKEY WITH WALNUT PESTO

1 (4 to 5½ lb.) turkey breast
Walnut Pesto Sauce

- Prepare coals for grilling.
- Place aluminum drip pan in center of charcoal grate under grilling rack. Arrange hot coals around drip pan.
- Place turkey on greased grill over hot coals (coals will be glowing). Grill, covered, 1½ to 2 hours or until internal temperature reaches 170°.
- Slice turkey; serve with Walnut Pesto Sauce. Garnish with red and yellow pear-shaped cherry tomatoes, fresh chives and basil leaves, if desired.   *12 servings*

WALNUT PESTO SAUCE

1 (8 oz.) container Light PHILADELPHIA BRAND Pasteurized Process Cream Cheese Product
1 (7 oz.) container refrigerated prepared pesto
½ cup finely chopped walnuts, toasted
⅓ cup milk
1 garlic clove, minced
⅛ teaspoon cayenne pepper

- Stir together all ingredients in small bowl until well blended. Serve chilled or at room temperature.

Prep time: 15 minutes
Cooking time: 2 hours

For a beautiful presentation, place fresh basil leaves between the turkey skin and meat. Use fingers to gently lift skin from meat, starting at the V-shaped end. Place basil leaves under skin on each side of the breast. (Do not puncture skin.) Return skin to original position. Rub surface lightly with vegetable oil.

50

Grilled Turkey with Walnut Pesto

FETTUCCINE WITH SUN-DRIED TOMATO CREAM

⅔ cup sun-dried tomatoes
3 to 4 garlic cloves
1 (8 oz.) container PHILADELPHIA
    BRAND Soft Cream Cheese
½ teaspoon dried oregano leaves,
    crushed
¼ cup PARKAY Margarine
¼ cup BREAKSTONE'S Sour Cream
1 lb. fettuccine, cooked, drained
¼ cup olive oil
    Salt and pepper
2 tablespoons chopped fresh parsley

- Cover tomatoes with boiling water; let stand 10 minutes. Drain.
- Place tomatoes and garlic in food processor or blender container; process until coarsely chopped. Add cream cheese and oregano; process until well blended.
- Melt margarine in medium saucepan; stir in cream cheese mixture and sour cream. Cook until thoroughly heated.
- Toss hot fettuccine with oil.
- Add cream cheese mixture. Season with salt and pepper to taste. Sprinkle with chopped parsley. Serve immediately.

8 to 10 servings

Prep time: 30 minutes

Sun-dried tomatoes can be purchased dried or packed in oil, usually olive oil. The dry-pack tomatoes, like good quality dried fruit, should be slightly moist to the touch.

OVEN-BAKED FRENCH TOAST WITH CRANBERRY MAPLE SAUCE

A great make-ahead brunch idea. Prepare this recipe as directed except for baking. Cover and refrigerate overnight. Uncover, then bake as directed.

1 (8 oz.) pkg. PHILADELPHIA
    BRAND Cream Cheese, softened
¾ cup sugar
¼ cup PARKAY Margarine
2 teaspoons vanilla
1 teaspoon ground cinnamon
4 eggs
2½ cups milk
1 (1 lb.) French bread loaf, cut into
    1½-inch slices
1 cup cranberries
    Cranberry Maple Sauce

- Preheat oven to 350°.
- Beat cream cheese, sugar, margarine, vanilla and cinnamon in large mixing bowl at medium speed with electric mixer until well blended. Add eggs, one at a time, mixing well after each addition. Stir in milk.
- Pour cream cheese mixture over combined bread and cranberries in large bowl; toss lightly. Let stand 15 minutes, rearranging bread in bowl occasionally to moisten evenly.
- Arrange bread in rows in greased 13×9-inch baking pan. Pour remaining cream cheese mixture over bread.
- Bake 40 to 45 minutes or until golden brown. Serve with Cranberry Maple Sauce. *10 to 12 servings*

CRANBERRY MAPLE SAUCE

1 cup LOG CABIN Syrup
2 cups cranberries
2 tablespoons sugar

- Bring syrup to boil in medium saucepan. Add cranberries and sugar.
- Cook over low heat 10 minutes, stirring occasionally. Cool slightly.

Prep time: 25 minutes plus standing
Cooking time: 45 minutes

52

STUFFED GRILLED GAME HENS

4 (1 to 1½ lbs. each) frozen Cornish game hens, thawed
½ cup orange juice
½ cup oil
1 garlic clove, minced
⅛ teaspoon pepper
1⅓ cups MINUTE Rice, uncooked
1 (8 oz.) container PHILADELPHIA BRAND Soft Cream Cheese
¼ cup golden raisins
¼ cup chopped fresh parsley
2 tablespoons orange juice
1 shallot, minced
1½ teaspoons grated orange peel
½ teaspoon salt
⅛ teaspoon pepper

- Remove giblets; discard or save for another use. Rinse hens; pat dry.
- Marinate hens in combined ½ cup orange juice, oil, garlic and ⅛ teaspoon pepper in refrigerator 30 minutes, basting occasionally.
- Prepare coals for grilling.
- Prepare rice according to package directions.
- Mix together rice with remaining ingredients in medium bowl.
- Remove hens from marinade. Stuff hens with rice mixture; close openings with skewers.
- Place aluminum drip pan in center of charcoal grate under grilling rack. Arrange hot coals around drip pan.
- Place hens, breast side up, on greased grill directly over drip pan. Grill, covered, 1 hour and 15 minutes to 1 hour and 30 minutes or until tender. Serve with cooked whole carrots, if desired.

4 servings

Prep time: 40 minutes plus marinating
Cooking time: 1 hour and 30 minutes

These Cornish game hens are grilled using the indirect heat method. This method is typically used for larger cuts of meat, enabling them to be cooked evenly on the grill. Here, the coals are placed around an aluminum drip pan. The food is then placed over the pan, not the hot coals. The food is always cooked under a covered grill, causing the heat to circulate around the food in a fashion similar to that used in an oven.

BRANDIED CHICKEN THIGHS WITH MUSHROOMS

Easy and elegant ... nothing could be better for informal entertaining.

2½ lbs. (8 to 10) chicken thighs
Flour
¼ cup PARKAY Margarine
2 cups mushroom slices
½ cup brandy
1 (8 oz.) container PHILADELPHIA BRAND Soft Cream Cheese with Herb & Garlic
Salt and pepper

- Lightly coat chicken with flour. Brown chicken in margarine in large skillet; remove chicken, reserving drippings in skillet.
- Sauté mushrooms in reserved drippings until tender. Stir in brandy. Return chicken to skillet. Cook, covered, 30 minutes or until tender. Place chicken on ovenproof serving platter. Cover; keep warm.
- Skim fat from drippings in skillet; discard fat. Add cream cheese to reserved drippings; stir until mixture is smooth and thoroughly heated. Season with salt and pepper to taste. Pour over chicken.

4 to 6 servings

Prep time: 50 minutes

53

Dazzling Desserts

CHOCOLATE PEANUT BUTTER SQUARES

1½ cups chocolate-covered graham
    cracker crumbs (approx.
    17 crackers)
3 tablespoons PARKAY Margarine,
    melted
1 (8 oz.) pkg. PHILADELPHIA
    BRAND Cream Cheese, softened
½ cup chunk-style peanut butter
1 cup powdered sugar
¼ cup BAKER'S Semi-Sweet Real
    Chocolate Chips
1 teaspoon shortening

- Preheat oven to 350°.
- Stir together crumbs and margarine in
  small bowl. Press onto bottom of 9-inch
  square baking pan. Bake 10 minutes.
  Cool.
- Beat cream cheese, peanut butter and
  sugar in small mixing bowl at medium
  speed with electric mixer until well
  blended. Spread over crust.
- Melt chocolate chips with shortening in
  small saucepan over low heat, stirring
  until smooth. Drizzle over cream cheese
  mixture. Chill 6 hours or overnight. Cut
  into squares.   *Approximately 1 dozen*

Prep time: 20 minutes plus chilling
Cooking time: 10 minutes

Microwave Tip: Microwave chocolate chips
and shortening in small bowl on HIGH 1 to
2 minutes or until chocolate begins to melt,
stirring every minute. Stir until chocolate is
completely melted.

SPRING FLING FRUIT TART

1 cup flour
¼ cup packed brown sugar
½ cup PARKAY Margarine
1 (8 oz.) pkg. PHILADELPHIA
    BRAND Cream Cheese, softened
¼ cup granulated sugar
1 tablespoon grated orange peel
¾ cup whipping cream, whipped
    Peeled kiwi slices
    Strawberry halves

- Preheat oven to 350°.
- Stir together flour and brown sugar in
  medium bowl. Cut in margarine until
  mixture resembles coarse crumbs; knead
  mixture until well blended. Press onto
  bottom and ½ inch up sides of 10-inch tart
  pan with removable bottom.
- Bake 15 minutes or until golden brown.
  Cool.
- Beat cream cheese, granulated sugar and
  peel in large mixing bowl at medium
  speed with electric mixer until well
  blended. Fold in whipped cream; pour into
  crust. Chill until firm.
- Arrange fruit on top of tart just before
  serving. Carefully remove rim of pan.
                        10 to 12 servings

Prep time: 30 minutes plus chilling

Tip: When preparing crust, wet fingertips in
cold water before pressing dough into pan.

54

Spring Fling Fruit Tart

FRUIT COBBLER

Quick and easy, this cobbler is made from convenient ingredients and can be baked in a skillet.

> 1 (21 oz.) can cherry pie filling
> 1 (17 oz.) can fruit cocktail in heavy syrup, undrained
> ¼ teaspoon almond extract
> 1 (3 oz.) pkg. PHILADELPHIA BRAND Cream Cheese, softened
> ½ cup sugar
> ⅓ cup PARKAY Margarine, melted
> 2 cups variety baking mix
> 1 tablespoon sugar
> ½ teaspoon ground cinnamon
> Honey Cream Cheese

- Preheat oven to 375°.
- Mix pie filling, fruit cocktail and extract; pour into 2-quart casserole or 10-inch cast-iron skillet.
- Mix cream cheese and ½ cup sugar until well blended; gradually stir in margarine. Stir in baking mix.
- Crumble cream cheese mixture over fruit mixture. Sprinkle with combined 1 tablespoon sugar and cinnamon.
- Bake 35 to 40 minutes or until golden brown. Serve warm with Honey Cream Cheese.   *8 to 10 servings*

HONEY CREAM CHEESE

> 1 (8 oz.) pkg. PHILADELPHIA BRAND Cream Cheese, softened
> 2 tablespoons honey
> 1 tablespoon rum or orange juice
> ¼ teaspoon ground nutmeg

- Mix cream cheese, honey, rum and nutmeg until well blended.

Prep time: 15 minutes
Cooking time: 40 minutes

APPLE CREAM CRUMBLE PIE

PHILLY Cream Cheese adds a rich creamy layer to this apple pie.

> ½ (15 oz.) pkg. refrigerated pie crusts (1 crust)
> 1 (8 oz.) pkg. PHILADELPHIA BRAND Cream Cheese, softened
> ⅓ cup sugar
> 1 teaspoon vanilla
> 1 egg
> ⅔ cup BREAKSTONE'S Sour Cream
> 3 apples, sliced
> ½ cup flour
> ¼ cup sugar
> 1 teaspoon ground cinnamon
> ⅓ cup PARKAY Margarine
> ½ cup chopped pecans

- Preheat oven to 350°.
- On lightly floured surface, roll pastry to 12-inch circle. Place in 10-inch quiche dish or tart pan with removable bottom. Trim edges of pastry even with top of dish. Prick bottom and sides of pastry with fork. Bake 15 minutes.
- Beat cream cheese, ⅓ cup sugar and vanilla in large mixing bowl at medium speed with electric mixer until well blended. Add egg; mix well. Blend in sour cream. Pour into crust. Top with apples.
- Mix together flour, ¼ cup sugar and cinnamon in medium bowl; cut in margarine until mixture resembles coarse crumbs. Stir in pecans; sprinkle over apples.
- Bake 50 minutes. Cool. Garnish with cinnamon sticks tied with orange peel, if desired.   *12 servings*

Prep time: 30 minutes
Cooking time: 50 minutes

56

Apple Cream Crumble Pie

LEMON CHEESECAKE SQUARES

1⅓ cups shortbread cookie crumbs
　　(approx. 18 cookies)
⅓ cup ground almonds
3 tablespoons PARKAY Margarine,
　　melted
2 tablespoons sugar
1 (6 oz.) container frozen lemonade
　　concentrate, thawed
3 (8 oz.) pkgs. PHILADELPHIA
　　BRAND Cream Cheese, softened
1 cup BREAKSTONE'S Sour Cream
1 (3½ oz.) pkg. JELL-O Brand Lemon
　　Flavor Instant Pudding and Pie
　　Filling
2 cups thawed COOL WHIP Whipped
　　Topping

- Preheat oven to 350°.
- Stir together crumbs, almonds, margarine and sugar in small bowl; press onto bottom of 13×9-inch baking pan. Bake 10 minutes. Cool.
- Gradually add lemonade concentrate to cream cheese in large mixing bowl, mixing at low speed with electric mixer until well blended. Add sour cream and pudding mix; beat 1 minute.
- Fold in whipped topping; pour over crust.
- Freeze until firm. Cut into squares.

18 servings

Prep time: 15 minutes plus freezing

58

BANANA BERRY BROWNIE PIZZA

A fresh fruit pizza with a brownie crust is a guaranteed success at any party.

⅓ cup cold water
1 (15 oz.) pkg. brownie mix
¼ cup oil
1 egg
1 (8 oz.) pkg. PHILADELPHIA
　　BRAND Cream Cheese, softened
¼ cup sugar
1 egg
1 teaspoon vanilla
　Strawberry slices
　Banana slices
2 (1 oz.) squares BAKER'S Semi-Sweet
　　Chocolate, melted

- Preheat oven to 350°.
- Bring water to boil.
- Mix together brownie mix, water, oil and one egg in large bowl until well blended.
- Pour into greased and floured 12-inch pizza pan.
- Bake 25 minutes.
- Beat cream cheese, sugar, remaining egg and vanilla in small mixing bowl at medium speed with electric mixer until well blended. Pour over crust.
- Continue baking 15 minutes. Cool. Top with fruit; drizzle with chocolate. Garnish with mint leaves, if desired.

10 to 12 servings

Prep time: 35 minutes
Cooking time: 40 minutes

Microwave Tip: To melt chocolate, place unwrapped chocolate squares in small bowl. Microwave on HIGH 1 to 2 minutes or until almost melted. Stir until chocolate is completely melted.

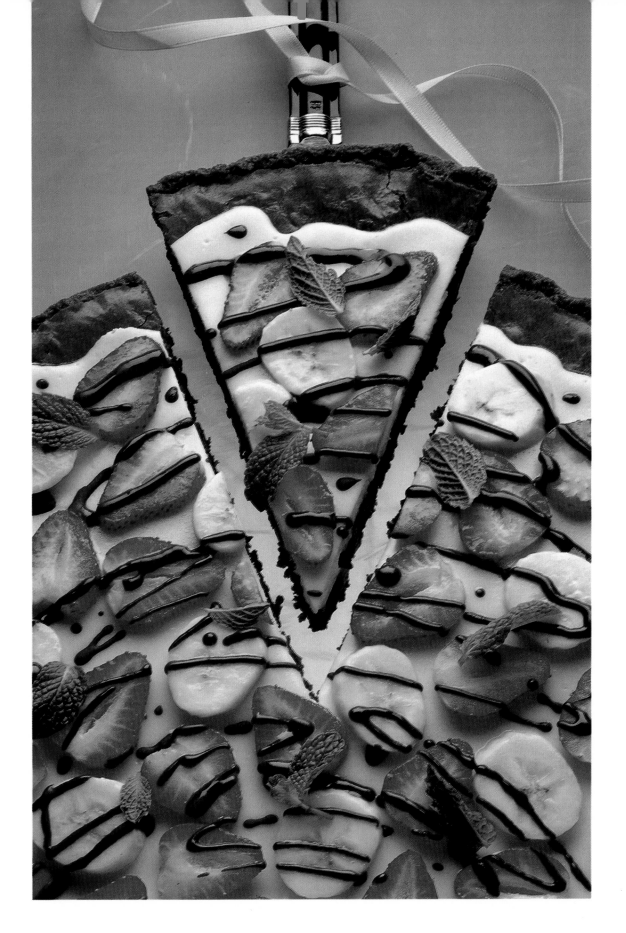

Banana Berry Brownie Pizza

WHITE MOUSSE WITH RASPBERRY SAUCE

This dessert can be made especially elegant when served as individual molded desserts.

> ½ cup milk
> 1 cup (8 ozs.) ready-to-spread vanilla frosting
> 1 envelope unflavored gelatin
> ¼ cup milk
> 1 (12 oz.) container PHILADELPHIA BRAND Soft Cream Cheese
> 2 teaspoons vanilla
> 2 egg whites, room temperature
> ¼ teaspoon salt
> ½ cup whipping cream
> Raspberry Sauce

- Mix together ½ cup milk and frosting in medium saucepan over low heat, stirring constantly. Remove from heat.
- Soften gelatin in ¼ cup milk in small saucepan; stir over low heat until dissolved. Add to frosting mixture; cool.
- Beat cream cheese and vanilla in large mixing bowl at medium speed with electric mixer until well blended. Blend in frosting mixture.
- Beat egg whites and salt in small mixing bowl at high speed with electric mixer until stiff peaks form. In separate bowl, beat whipping cream at high speed with electric mixer until stiff peaks form.
- Fold egg whites and whipped cream into cream cheese mixture.
- Pour into lightly oiled 1½- to 2-quart mold; chill until firm. Unmold; serve with Raspberry Sauce.   *14 to 16 servings*

RASPBERRY SAUCE

> 1 (10 oz.) pkg. BIRDS EYE Quick Thaw Red Raspberries in a Lite Syrup, thawed
> ½ cup KRAFT Red Currant Jelly
> 4 teaspoons cornstarch

- Place raspberries and jelly in food processor or blender container; process until well blended. Strain.
- Stir together cornstarch and raspberry mixture in small saucepan until smooth.
- Bring to boil over medium heat, stirring constantly. Cook until thickened, stirring constantly. Cool.

Prep time: 25 minutes plus chilling
Cooking time: 10 minutes

Microwave Tip: To dissolve gelatin, soften gelatin in milk. Microwave on HIGH 30 to 45 seconds or until dissolved, stirring every 15 seconds.

WALNUT SHORTBREAD BARS

> 1 (8 oz.) pkg. PHILADELPHIA BRAND Cream Cheese, softened
> 1 cup PARKAY Margarine
> ¾ cup granulated sugar
> ¾ cup packed brown sugar
> 1 egg
> 1 teaspoon vanilla
> 2½ cups flour
> 1 teaspoon CALUMET Baking Powder
> ½ teaspoon salt
> ¾ cup chopped walnuts

- Preheat oven to 350°.
- Beat cream cheese, margarine and sugars in large mixing bowl at medium speed with electric mixer until well blended. Blend in egg and vanilla.
- Add combined dry ingredients; mix well. Stir in walnuts. Spread into greased 15×10×1-inch jelly roll pan.
- Bake 20 to 25 minutes or until lightly browned. Cool. Sprinkle with powdered sugar just before serving, if desired. Cut into bars.   *Approximately 5 dozen*

Prep time: 15 minutes
Cooking time: 25 minutes

61

BLUEBERRY PEAR CREAM CHEESE CRISP

A perfect dessert for a crowd.

  2 cups old-fashioned or quick oats, uncooked
  1 cup flour
  ⅓ cup granulated sugar
  ⅓ cup packed brown sugar
  ½ cup PARKAY Margarine, melted
  2 (8 oz.) containers Light PHILADELPHIA BRAND Pasteurized Process Cream Cheese Product
  ½ cup granulated sugar
  2 eggs
  2 tablespoons lemon juice
  1 tablespoon grated lemon peel
  2 pears, peeled, cored, sliced, halved
  1 pt. blueberries

- Preheat oven to 325°.
- Mix together oats, flour, ⅓ cup granulated sugar and brown sugar in medium bowl until well blended. Stir in margarine.
- Reserve 1 cup oat mixture for topping. Press remaining oat mixture onto bottom of 13×9-inch baking pan. Bake 10 minutes.
- Beat cream cheese product and ½ cup granulated sugar in large mixing bowl at medium speed with electric mixer until well blended. Add eggs, one at a time, mixing well after each addition. Blend in lemon juice and peel; pour over crust.
- Layer pears evenly over cream cheese mixture; top with blueberries. Sprinkle reserved oat mixture over fruit.
- Bake 45 minutes. Serve warm with vanilla ice cream, if desired.   *16 servings*

Prep time: 20 minutes
Cooking time: 45 minutes

ORANGE POPPY SEED CAKE

  1 (8 oz.) container Light PHILADELPHIA BRAND Pasteurized Process Cream Cheese Product
  ½ cup PARKAY Margarine
  1 cup granulated sugar
  3 eggs, separated
  2 cups flour
  1 teaspoon CALUMET Baking Powder
  1 teaspoon baking soda
  1 cup BREAKSTONE'S LIGHT CHOICE Sour Half and Half
  2 tablespoons poppy seeds
  1 tablespoon grated orange peel
  ½ cup granulated sugar
  ⅓ cup orange-flavored liqueur
  ¼ cup orange juice
  3 tablespoons powdered sugar

- Preheat oven to 350°.
- Beat cream cheese product, margarine and 1 cup granulated sugar in large mixing bowl at medium speed with electric mixer until well blended. Beat in egg yolks.
- Mix together flour, baking powder and soda; add to cream cheese mixture alternately with sour half and half. Stir in poppy seeds and peel.
- Beat egg whites in small mixing bowl at high speed with electric mixer until stiff peaks form; fold into cream cheese mixture. Pour into greased 10-inch fluted tube pan.
- Bake 50 minutes.
- Stir together ½ cup sugar, liqueur and orange juice in saucepan over low heat until sugar dissolves.
- Prick hot cake several times with fork. Pour syrup over cake; cool 10 minutes. Invert onto serving plate. Cool completely. Sprinkle with powdered sugar just before serving. Garnish with quartered orange slices, if desired.   *16 servings*

Prep time: 30 minutes
Cooking time: 50 minutes

Variation: Omit orange-flavored liqueur. Increase orange juice to ½ cup.

62

Orange Poppy Seed Cake

NAPOLEONS

1 frozen ready-to-bake puff pastry
sheet
1 (8 oz.) container PHILADELPHIA
BRAND Soft Cream Cheese
¼ **cup powdered sugar**
¼ **teaspoon almond extract**
1 cup whipping cream, whipped
½ **cup powdered sugar**
1 tablespoon milk
1 (1 oz.) square BAKER'S Semi-Sweet
Chocolate, melted

- Thaw puff pastry sheet according to package directions.
- Preheat oven to 400°.
- On lightly floured surface, roll pastry to 15×12-inch rectangle. Cut lengthwise into thirds.
- Place pastry strips on large ungreased cookie sheet; prick pastry generously with fork. Bake 8 to 10 minutes or until light golden brown.
- Stir together cream cheese, ¼ cup sugar and extract in medium bowl until well blended. Fold in whipped cream.
- Spread two pastry strips with cream cheese mixture; stack. Top with remaining pastry strip.
- Stir together ½ cup sugar and milk in small bowl until smooth. Spread over top pastry strip. Drizzle with melted chocolate. Chill.   *10 servings*

Prep time: 20 minutes plus chilling
Cooking time: 10 minutes

Microwave Tip: Microwave chocolate in small bowl on HIGH 30 seconds to 1 minute or until chocolate begins to melt, stirring every 30 seconds. Stir until chocolate is completely melted.

64

BISCOTTI

Italian tradition calls for dunking these crisp cookies in wine or coffee.

1 (8 oz.) pkg. PHILADELPHIA
BRAND Cream Cheese, softened
¾ **cup PARKAY Margarine**
¾ **cup sugar**
1 teaspoon vanilla
½ **teaspoon anise extract**
4 eggs
3¼ **cups flour**
1 teaspoon CALUMET Baking Powder
⅛ **teaspoon salt**
½ **cup sliced almonds, toasted**

- Preheat oven to 400°.
- Beat cream cheese, margarine, sugar, vanilla and extract in large mixing bowl at medium speed with electric mixer until well blended. Blend in eggs.
- Gradually add combined dry ingredients; mix well. Stir in almonds.
- On well-floured surface with floured hands, shape dough into three 12×1½-inch logs. Place logs, 2 inches apart, on greased and floured cookie sheet.
- Bake 15 to 20 minutes or until light golden brown. (Dough will spread and flatten slightly during baking.) Cool slightly.
- Diagonally cut each log into ¾-inch slices. Place on cookie sheet.
- Continue baking 5 to 10 minutes or until light golden brown. Cool on wire rack.
                    3 dozen

Prep time: 15 minutes
Cooking time: 30 minutes

Variation: Substitute almond or lemon extract for anise extract.

STRAWBERRY COOKIE TARTS

These tasty treats are best eaten the day they are made.

  1 (20 oz.) pkg. refrigerated sliceable
    sugar cookie dough
  2 (8 oz.) containers PHILADELPHIA
    BRAND Soft Cream Cheese with
    Strawberries
  ¼ cup powdered sugar
  ¼ cup BAKER'S Semi-Sweet Real
    Chocolate Chips
  1 teaspoon shortening

• Preheat oven to 325°.
• Slice cookie dough into thirty-six ¼-inch slices. Place on bottom and ¼ inch up sides of well-greased medium-size muffin pan.
• Bake 12 to 15 minutes or until edges are golden brown. Cool 5 minutes; remove from pan. Cool completely.
• Stir together cream cheese and sugar in medium bowl until well blended. Spoon into tarts.
• Melt chocolate chips with shortening in small saucepan over low heat, stirring until smooth. Drizzle over cream cheese mixture.   *3 dozen*

Prep time: 25 minutes
Cooking time: 15 minutes

Variation: Spoon cream cheese mixture into pastry bag fitted with large star tip. Pipe mixture into tarts.

LEMON NUT BARS

  1⅓ cups flour
  ½ cup packed brown sugar
  ¼ cup granulated sugar
  ¾ cup PARKAY Margarine
  1 cup old-fashioned or quick oats,
    uncooked
  ½ cup chopped nuts
  1 (8 oz.) pkg. PHILADELPHIA
    BRAND Cream Cheese, softened
  1 egg
  3 tablespoons lemon juice
  1 tablespoon grated lemon peel

• Preheat oven to 350°.
• Stir together flour and sugars in medium bowl. Cut in margarine until mixture resembles coarse crumbs. Stir in oats and nuts.
• Reserve 1 cup crumb mixture; press remaining crumb mixture onto bottom of greased 13×9-inch baking pan. Bake 15 minutes.
• Beat cream cheese, egg, juice and peel in small mixing bowl at medium speed with electric mixer until well blended. Pour over crust; sprinkle with reserved crumb mixture.
• Bake 25 minutes. Cool; cut into bars.
                    Approximately 3 dozen

Prep time: 30 minutes
Cooking time: 25 minutes

RASPBERRY CHOCOLATE FONDUE

  ½ cup KRAFT Red Raspberry Preserves
  1 (8 oz.) container PHILADELPHIA
    BRAND Soft Cream Cheese
  1 cup BAKER'S Semi-Sweet Real
    Chocolate Chips
  2 tablespoons raspberry-flavored
    liqueur

• Heat preserves in small saucepan until softened; strain.
• Mix together preserves and cream cheese in small bowl until smooth.
• Melt chocolate chips with liqueur in medium saucepan over low heat, stirring until smooth.
• Gradually add cream cheese mixture, beating with wire whisk until smooth and thoroughly heated. Serve warm with cake cubes, banana slices or orange sections.
                    1⅓ cups

Prep time: 20 minutes

GERMAN SWEET CHOCOLATE CREAM CHEESE BROWNIES

1 (4 oz.) pkg. BAKER'S GERMAN'S Sweet Chocolate
¼ cup PARKAY Margarine
¾ cup sugar
2 eggs, beaten
1 teaspoon vanilla
½ cup flour
½ cup chopped nuts
4 ozs. PHILADELPHIA BRAND Cream Cheese, softened
¼ cup sugar
1 egg
1 tablespoon flour

- Preheat oven to 350°.
- Microwave chocolate and margarine in large bowl on HIGH 2 minutes or until margarine is melted. Stir until chocolate is completely melted.
- Add ¾ cup sugar; mix well. Blend in two eggs and vanilla. Stir in ½ cup flour and nuts; mix well. Spread into greased 8-inch square baking pan.
- In small bowl, mix cream cheese and remaining sugar, egg and flour until well blended. Spoon over brownie mixture; cut through batter with knife several times for marble effect.
- Bake 35 to 40 minutes or until wooden pick inserted in center comes out almost clean. (*Do not overbake.*) Cool. Cut into squares.   *16 servings*

Prep time: 15 minutes
Cooking time: 40 minutes

Conventional: Melt chocolate and margarine in 2-quart saucepan over low heat; stir constantly just until melted. Remove from heat. Continue as directed.

HOLIDAY PEPPERMINT CANDIES

One batch of these creamy candies goes a long way. Give some as gifts and keep some to enjoy yourself.

4 ozs. PHILADELPHIA BRAND Cream Cheese, softened
1 tablespoon PARKAY Margarine
1 tablespoon light corn syrup
¼ teaspoon peppermint extract or few drops peppermint oil
4 cups powdered sugar
Green and red food coloring
Sifted powdered sugar
Green, red and white decorating icing (optional)

- Beat cream cheese, margarine, corn syrup and extract in large mixing bowl at medium speed with electric mixer until well blended. Gradually add 4 cups powdered sugar; mix well.
- Divide mixture into thirds. Knead few drops green food coloring into one third; repeat with red food coloring and second third. Wrap each third in plastic wrap.
- Working with one color mixture at a time, shape into ¾-inch balls. Place on waxed paper-lined cookie sheet. Flatten each ball with bottom of glass that has been lightly dipped in sugar.
- Repeat with remaining mixtures. Decorate with icing. Chill.   *5 dozen*

Prep time: 30 minutes plus chilling

66

Holiday Peppermint Candies

CUSTARD BREAD PUDDING

2 (8 oz.) pkgs. PHILADELPHIA
    BRAND Cream Cheese, softened
½ cup packed brown sugar
1 teaspoon vanilla
1 teaspoon grated lemon peel
2½ cups milk
3 eggs, beaten
2 tablespoons whiskey or brandy
8 cups stale cinnamon-raisin bread
    cubes

- Beat cream cheese, sugar, vanilla and peel in large mixing bowl at medium speed with electric mixer until well blended. Gradually add milk, eggs and whiskey; mix well.
- Place bread in large bowl. Pour cream cheese mixture over bread; mix well. Let stand 30 minutes, stirring occasionally.
- Preheat oven to 325°.
- Pour mixture into greased 2-quart casserole; cover.
- Bake 40 minutes. Uncover; continue baking 35 minutes. Let stand at least 1 hour before serving. Serve with half and half or milk.   *10 to 12 servings*

Prep time: 10 minutes plus standing
Cooking time: 1 hour and 15 minutes

ALMOND AMARETTO DESSERT

1 (8 oz.) container Light
    PHILADELPHIA BRAND
    Pasteurized Process Cream Cheese
    Product
2 cups skim milk
1 (9 oz.) pkg. JELL-O Vanilla Flavor
    Sugar Free Instant Pudding and
    Pie Filling
3 tablespoons almond-flavored liqueur
1 (1.65 oz.) milk chocolate bar, grated
2 cups COOL WHIP Whipped Topping,
    thawed
⅓ cup sliced almonds, toasted

- Blend cream cheese product and ½ cup milk in large mixing bowl at low speed with electric mixer until well blended.
- Whisk together remaining milk with pudding mix in medium bowl until well blended. Add to cream cheese mixture; mix well. Stir in liqueur; pour into 1½-quart straight-sided glass bowl. Chill.
- Sprinkle half of grated chocolate over cream cheese mixture. Spoon whipped topping over chocolate. Sprinkle with almonds and remaining chocolate.
                                    8 servings

Prep time: 30 minutes plus chilling

COFFEE TOFFEE PIE

2 cups chocolate wafer crumbs
    (approx. 40 wafers)
¼ cup sugar
6 tablespoons PARKAY Margarine,
    melted
1 (8 oz.) pkg. PHILADELPHIA
    BRAND Cream Cheese, softened
3 to 4 tablespoons coffee-flavored
    liqueur
1 (8 oz.) container COOL WHIP
    Whipped Topping, thawed
4 (1.4 ozs. each) milk chocolate-
    covered toffee bars, chopped
    (approx. 1 cup)

- Preheat oven to 350°.
- Stir together crumbs, sugar and margarine in medium bowl; press onto bottom and up sides of 9-inch pie plate. Bake 10 minutes.
- Beat cream cheese and liqueur in large mixing bowl at medium speed with electric mixer until well blended. Fold in whipped topping and ¾ cup candy; pour into crust.
- Sprinkle with remaining candy. Chill until firm.   *8 to 10 servings*

Prep time: 15 minutes plus chilling

68

69

Coffee Toffee Pie

PHILLY MANDARIN DESSERT

1 (1.3 oz.) pkg. DREAM WHIP
   Whipped Topping Mix
½ cup cold skim milk
1 teaspoon vanilla
1 (11 oz.) can mandarin orange
   segments, undrained
1 (3 oz.) pkg. JELL-O Brand Orange
   Flavor Sugar Free Gelatin
½ cup cold water
1 (8 oz.) pkg. Light PHILADELPHIA
   BRAND Neufchatel Cheese,
   softened
1 (8 oz.) container exotic fruit- or
   lemon-flavored yogurt
½ cup BAKER'S ANGEL FLAKE
   Coconut, toasted

- Beat topping mix, milk and vanilla in small mixing bowl at high speed with electric mixer until soft peaks form. Chill.
- Drain orange segments, reserving syrup; pour syrup into small saucepan. Bring syrup to boil. Dissolve gelatin in syrup; add water. Chill until thickened but not set.
- Beat neufchatel cheese and yogurt in large mixing bowl at medium speed with electric mixer until well blended. Gradually add gelatin mixture. Chill 15 minutes.
- Fold orange segments and whipped topping into neufchatel cheese mixture. Spoon into individual serving dishes. Chill until firm. Sprinkle with coconut.

6 to 8 servings

Prep time: 25 minutes plus chilling

HOLIDAY CHARLOTTE RUSSE

For an elegant presentation, tie a colorful ribbon around this festive dessert.

18 ladyfingers, split
 2 tablespoons rum (optional)
1½ teaspoons unflavored gelatin
 3 cups eggnog
 2 (8 oz.) pkgs. PHILADELPHIA
   BRAND Cream Cheese, softened
 2 (3½ oz.) pkgs. JELL-O Vanilla Flavor
   Instant Pudding and Pie Filling
 1 teaspoon rum extract
¼ teaspoon ground nutmeg
 1 cup whole berry cranberry sauce

- Place ladyfingers, cut sides in, on bottom and around sides of 9-inch springform pan; sprinkle with rum.
- Soften gelatin in ¼ cup eggnog in medium saucepan; stir over low heat 5 minutes or until dissolved. Stir in remaining 2¾ cups eggnog.
- Beat cream cheese in large mixing bowl at medium speed with electric mixer until smooth. Add eggnog mixture alternately with pudding mix, mixing well after each addition. Stir in extract and nutmeg.
- Pour into ladyfinger-lined springform pan. Chill 8 hours or overnight.
- Loosen ladyfingers from rim of pan; remove rim. Top with cranberry sauce just before serving. Garnish with ribbon, if desired. *10 to 12 servings*

Prep time: 15 minutes plus chilling

70

Holiday Charlotte Russe

SUGARED CRÈME BRÛLÉE

The use of a water bath helps prevent the custard mixture from overcooking and curdling.

¼ cup PARKAY Margarine
½ cup packed brown sugar
1 tablespoon cold water
1 (8 oz.) pkg. PHILADELPHIA
   BRAND Cream Cheese, softened
⅓ cup packed brown sugar
2 teaspoons vanilla
6 eggs
2 cups half and half

- Preheat oven to 350°.
- Melt margarine in small saucepan. Stir in ½ cup sugar and water. Cook over medium heat 2 minutes or until well blended, stirring constantly. Spoon into eight (6-ounce) custard cups.
- Beat cream cheese, ⅓ cup sugar and vanilla in large mixing bowl at medium speed with electric mixer until well blended.
- Add eggs, one at a time, mixing well after each addition. Blend in half and half.
- Pour over sugar mixture in custard cups. Place cups in large shallow baking pan. Place baking pan on oven rack; carefully pour boiling water into baking pan to ½-inch depth.
- Bake 35 to 40 minutes or until center is set and knife inserted near centers comes out clean.
- Remove cups from water immediately; cool 5 minutes. Unmold onto serving plates. *8 servings*

Prep time: 15 minutes
Cooking time: 40 minutes

CHEESECAKE MACAROON BARS

These bars are a great treat for afternoon tea, brunch or a casual party.

1 cup flour
1 cup ground almonds
½ cup PARKAY Margarine
⅓ cup packed brown sugar
¼ teaspoon salt
¼ teaspoon almond extract
2 (8 oz.) pkgs. PHILADELPHIA
   BRAND Cream Cheese, softened
¾ cup granulated sugar
1 tablespoon lemon juice
3 eggs
1 cup BAKER'S ANGEL FLAKE
   Coconut, toasted
1½ cups BREAKSTONE'S Sour Cream
3 tablespoons granulated sugar
2 teaspoons vanilla
½ cup BAKER'S ANGEL FLAKE
   Coconut, toasted

- Preheat oven to 350°.
- Beat flour, almonds, margarine, brown sugar, salt and extract in small mixing bowl at medium speed with electric mixer until well blended. Press onto bottom of 13×9-inch baking pan.
- Bake 8 to 10 minutes or until lightly browned.
- Beat cream cheese, ¾ cup granulated sugar and lemon juice in large mixing bowl at medium speed with electric mixer until well blended.
- Add eggs, one at a time, mixing well after each addition. Stir in 1 cup coconut; pour over crust.
- Bake 25 minutes. Cool 5 minutes.
- Stir together sour cream, 3 tablespoons granulated sugar and vanilla in small bowl until smooth; carefully spread over coconut mixture.
- Bake 5 to 7 minutes or until set. Sprinkle with ½ cup coconut; cool. Cut into bars. *Approximately 3 dozen*

Prep time: 30 minutes plus cooling
Cooking time: 32 minutes

72

Cheesecake Macaroon Bars

74

PHILLY CREAM CHEESE COOKIE DOUGH

1 (8 oz.) pkg. PHILADELPHIA
    BRAND Cream Cheese, softened
¾ cup butter
1 cup powdered sugar
2¼ cups flour
½ teaspoon baking soda

- Beat cream cheese, butter and sugar in large mixing bowl at medium speed with electric mixer until well blended.
- Add flour and soda; mix well.

3 cups dough

Chocolate Mint Cutouts:

- Preheat oven to 325°.
- Add ¼ teaspoon mint extract and few drops green food coloring to 1½ cups Cookie Dough; mix well. Chill 30 minutes.
- On lightly floured surface, roll dough to ⅛-inch thickness; cut with assorted 3-inch cookie cutters. Place on ungreased cookie sheet.
- Bake 10 to 12 minutes or until edges begin to brown. Cool on wire rack.
- Melt ¼ cup mint-flavored semisweet chocolate chips in small saucepan over low heat, stirring until smooth. Drizzle over cookies.

Approximately 3 dozen

Prep time: 20 minutes plus chilling
Cooking time: 12 minutes per batch

Variation: Sprinkle cookies with nonpareils before baking.

Snowmen:

- Preheat oven to 325°.
- Add ¼ teaspoon vanilla to 1½ cups Cookie Dough; mix well. Chill 30 minutes.
- For each snowman, shape dough into two small balls, one slightly larger than the other. Place balls, slightly overlapping, on ungreased cookie sheet; flatten with bottom of glass. Repeat with remaining dough.
- Bake 18 to 20 minutes or until edges begin to brown. Cool on wire rack.
- Sprinkle each snowman with sifted powdered sugar. Decorate with icing as desired. Cut miniature peanut butter cups in half for hats.

Approximately 2 dozen

Prep time: 15 minutes plus chilling and decorating
Cooking time: 20 minutes per batch

Choco-Orange Slices:

- Preheat oven to 325°.
- Add 1½ teaspoons grated orange peel to 1½ cups Cookie Dough; mix well. Shape into 8×1½-inch log. Chill 30 minutes.
- Cut log into ¼-inch slices. Place on ungreased cookie sheet.
- Bake 15 to 18 minutes or until edges begin to brown. Cool on wire rack.
- Melt ⅓ cup BAKER'S Semi-Sweet Real Chocolate Chips with 1 tablespoon orange juice and 1 tablespoon orange-flavored liqueur in small saucepan over low heat, stirring until smooth. Dip cookies into chocolate mixture.

Approximately 2½ dozen

Prep time: 15 minutes plus chilling
Cooking time: 18 minutes per batch

Preserve Thumbprints:

- Preheat oven to 325°.
- Add ½ cup chopped pecans and ½ teaspoon vanilla to 1½ cups Cookie Dough; mix well. Chill 30 minutes.
- Shape dough into 1-inch balls. Place on ungreased cookie sheet. Indent centers; fill each with 1 teaspoon KRAFT Preserves.
- Bake 14 to 16 minutes or until edges begin to brown. Cool on wire rack.

3½ dozen

Prep time: 15 minutes plus chilling
Cooking time: 16 minutes per batch

*Clockwise from top left: Preserve Thumbprints;
Snowmen; Choco-Orange Slices; Chocolate Mint Cutouts*

AMARETTO BREEZE

Easy elegance ... for a refreshing change, serve the sauce with melon balls, raspberries, sliced peaches or a combination of these fruits.

> 1 (8 oz.) pkg. PHILADELPHIA
>   BRAND Cream Cheese, softened
> ½ cup BREAKSTONE'S Sour Cream
> ½ cup sugar
> 3 tablespoons almond-flavored liqueur
> 2 tablespoons whipping cream
> 1 pt. blackberries or blueberries
> 1 pt. strawberries

- Beat cream cheese and sour cream in small mixing bowl at medium speed with electronic mixer until well blended. Blend in sugar, liqueur and cream. Chill.
- Place berries in individual serving dishes; top with cream cheese sauce.

4 to 6 servings

Prep time: 10 minutes plus chilling

FROZEN BANANA BOMBE

Be sure to remove dessert from freezer 30 minutes before serving.

> 1 (20 oz.) can crushed pineapple in
>   unsweetened juice, undrained
> 1 (8 oz.) pkg. Light PHILADELPHIA
>   BRAND Neufchatel Cheese,
>   softened
> 3 bananas
> ¼ teaspoon ground nutmeg
> 1 cup vanilla ice milk
> 3 bananas, sliced
> ¼ cup BAKER'S ANGEL FLAKE
>   Coconut, toasted

- Drain pineapple, reserving 3 tablespoons juice.
- Place neufchatel cheese, pineapple, reserved juice, three bananas and nutmeg in food processor or blender container; process until blended. Add ice milk; process until well blended.
- Fold in banana slices and coconut; pour into lightly oiled 8-cup mold or bowl. Freeze 4 to 6 hours or until firm.
- Remove from freezer 30 minutes before serving; unmold. Serve with KRAFT Hot Fudge Topping, if desired. *8 servings*

Prep time: 30 minutes plus freezing and standing

CHILLED LEMONADE DESSERT

> 1½ cups cold water
> 1 (3 oz.) pkg. JELL-O Brand Lemon
>   Flavor Sugar Free Gelatin
> 1 (8 oz.) pkg. Light PHILADELPHIA
>   BRAND Neufchatel Cheese,
>   softened
> ⅓ cup frozen lemonade concentrate,
>   thawed
> 1 teaspoon grated lemon peel
> 2 cups thawed COOL WHIP Whipped
>   Topping

- Bring water to boil. Gradually add to gelatin in small bowl; stir until dissolved.
- Beat neufchatel cheese, lemonade concentrate and peel in large mixing bowl at medium speed with electric mixer until well blended. Stir in gelatin; chill until thickened but not set.
- Fold in whipped topping; pour into lightly oiled 6-cup mold. Chill until firm. Unmold. Garnish with peach slices, blueberries and fresh mint leaves, if desired. *8 servings*

Prep time: 15 minutes plus chilling

Variation: Substitute eight individual ½-cup molds for 6-cup mold.

LAYERED FROZEN MOUSSE TORTE

For variety, substitute your favorite flavor premium ice cream for coffee ice cream.

  1½ cups chocolate wafer crumbs
       (approx. 30 wafers)
  6 tablespoons PARKAY Margarine,
       melted
  2 tablespoons sugar
  2 tablespoons PARKAY Margarine
  2 tablespoons sugar
  1 cup chopped almonds
  ½ cup cold water
  ¾ cup sugar
  1 (8 oz.) pkg. PHILADELPHIA
       BRAND Cream Cheese, softened
  6 (1 oz.) squares BAKER'S Semi-Sweet
       Chocolate, melted
  1½ cups whipping cream, whipped
  1 pt. premium coffee ice cream

- Preheat oven to 350°.
- Stir together crumbs, 6 tablespoons margarine and 2 tablespoons sugar in small bowl; press onto bottom and 2 inches up sides of 9-inch springform pan. Bake 10 minutes.
- Meanwhile, melt 2 tablespoons margarine in medium skillet over medium heat. Stir in 2 tablespoons sugar and almonds; cook 1 minute. Reduce heat to low; continue cooking almonds until golden brown, stirring constantly.
- Spread hot almond mixture over hot crust; press down lightly. Cool.
- Stir together water and ¾ cup sugar in small saucepan. Bring to boil; reduce heat to medium. Simmer 3 minutes.
- Beat cream cheese in large mixing bowl at medium speed with electric mixer until smooth. Gradually add sugar mixture, scraping bowl as needed. Blend in chocolate. Fold in whipped cream.
- Spread half of chocolate mixture over almond mixture. Refrigerate remaining chocolate mixture. Place springform pan in freezer 2 hours or until chocolate mixture is firm.

- Soften ice cream to spreading consistency. Spread over frozen chocolate layer; top with remaining chocolate mixture.
- Freeze several hours or overnight. Let stand at room temperature 10 to 15 minutes before serving.

10 to 12 servings

Prep time: 40 minutes plus freezing

STRAWBERRY COOL

  1 (10 oz.) pkg. BIRDS EYE Quick
       Thaw Strawberries in Syrup,
       partially thawed
  ¼ cup whipping cream
  1 (8 oz.) container PHILADELPHIA
       BRAND Soft Cream Cheese with
       Strawberries
  1 cup coarsely crumbled pecan
       shortbread cookies (approx.
       8 cookies)

- Place strawberries and whipping cream in food processor or blender container; process until well blended.
- Blend in cream cheese.
- Alternately layer cookie crumbs and strawberry mixture in individual parfait or sherbet glasses. Chill. Top with additional whipped cream, if desired.

4 servings

Prep time: 10 minutes plus chilling

Our Most Popular
Cheesecakes

ALMOND CHEESECAKE WITH RASPBERRIES

This quick and easy dessert can be prepared in advance for elegant entertaining.

1¼ cups graham cracker crumbs
¼ cup PARKAY Margarine, melted
¼ cup sugar
2 (8 oz.) pkgs. PHILADELPHIA BRAND Cream Cheese, softened
1 (16 oz.) can ready-to-spread vanilla frosting
1 tablespoon lemon juice
1 tablespoon grated lemon peel
3 cups thawed COOL WHIP Whipped Topping
Raspberries
Sliced almonds

• Stir together crumbs, margarine and sugar in small bowl; press onto bottom and ½ inch up sides of 9-inch springform pan or pie plate. Chill.
• Beat cream cheese, frosting, juice and peel in large mixing bowl at medium speed with electric mixer until well blended.
• Fold in whipped topping; pour into crust. Chill until firm.
• Carefully remove rim of pan just before serving. Arrange raspberries and almonds on top of cheesecake. Garnish with fresh mint leaves, if desired.

10 to 12 servings

Prep time: 30 minutes plus chilling

COOKIES 'N' CREAM CHEESECAKE

Everyone will love the cookies and cream combination—it's sure to be a hit!

1 cup chocolate sandwich cookie crumbs (approx. 12 cookies)
1 tablespoon PARKAY Margarine, melted
3 (8 oz.) pkgs. PHILADELPHIA BRAND Cream Cheese, softened
1 cup sugar
2 tablespoons flour
1 teaspoon vanilla
3 eggs
1 cup coarsely chopped chocolate sandwich cookies (approx. 8 cookies)

• Preheat oven to 325°.
• Mix together crumbs and margarine in small bowl. Press onto bottom of 9-inch springform pan. Bake 10 minutes.
• Beat cream cheese, sugar, flour and vanilla in large mixing bowl at medium speed with electric mixer until well blended.
• Add eggs, one at a time, mixing well after each addition. Fold in chopped cookies. Pour over crust.
• Bake 1 hour and 5 minutes. Loosen cake from rim of pan; cool before removing rim of pan. Chill. Garnish with thawed COOL WHIP Whipped Topping, chocolate sandwich cookies, cut in half, and fresh mint leaves, if desired.

10 to 12 servings

Prep time: 25 minutes plus chilling
Cooking time: 1 hour and 5 minutes

79

Cookies 'n' Cream Cheesecake

SAVANNAH PEACH CHEESECAKE

Another great cheesecake using PHILLY Cream Cheese.

    1 cup graham cracker crumbs
    3 tablespoons PARKAY Margarine,
        melted
    2 tablespoons sugar or 3 packets sugar
        substitute
    1 envelope unflavored gelatin
    ½ cup cold water
    1 (8 oz.) container Light
        PHILADELPHIA BRAND
        Pasteurized Process Cream Cheese
        Product
    3 tablespoons sugar or 4 packets sugar
        substitute
    ⅛ teaspoon ground ginger
    ½ cup skim milk
    2 (8 oz.) containers peach lowfat yogurt
    2 fresh peaches, pitted, peeled, sliced
    1 tablespoon lemon juice

- Stir together crumbs, margarine and 2 tablespoons sugar in small bowl; press onto bottom of 9-inch springform pan. Chill.
- Soften gelatin in water in small saucepan; stir over low heat until dissolved.
- Blend cream cheese product, 3 tablespoons sugar and ginger in large mixing bowl at medium speed with electric mixer until well blended. Gradually add gelatin and milk; mix well. Chill until mixture is thickened but not set.
- Fold in yogurt; pour over crust. Chill until firm.
- Carefully remove rim of pan just before serving. Toss together peach slices and lemon juice; drain. Arrange peaches on top of cheesecake.   *8 servings*

Prep time: 30 minutes plus chilling

MARBLE CHEESECAKE SQUARES

    1 cup flour
    1 cup chopped hazelnuts
    ½ cup PARKAY Margarine
    ⅓ cup packed brown sugar
    ¼ teaspoon almond extract
    3 (8 oz.) pkgs. PHILADELPHIA
        BRAND Cream Cheese, softened
    ¾ cup granulated sugar
    1 tablespoon orange-flavored liqueur
    1 teaspoon vanilla
    3 eggs
    1 (1 oz.) square BAKER'S Unsweetened
        Chocolate, melted

- Preheat oven to 325°.
- Beat flour, hazelnuts, margarine, brown sugar and extract in small mixing bowl at medium speed with electric mixer until well blended. Press onto bottom of 9-inch square baking pan. Bake 8 to 10 minutes or until lightly browned.
- Beat cream cheese, granulated sugar, liqueur and vanilla in large mixing bowl at medium speed with electric mixer until well blended.
- Add eggs, one at a time, mixing well after each addition.
- Blend melted chocolate into 1 cup batter; pour remaining batter over crust. Place chocolate batter in pastry tube. Pipe six strips on top of batter; cut through batter with knife several times for marble effect.
- Bake 30 to 35 minutes or until set. Chill.
                                     15 servings

Prep time: 15 minutes plus chilling
Cooking time: 35 minutes

◆◆◆

To soften cream cheese, microwave unwrapped packages in bowl on MEDIUM (50%) 30 seconds for each 8-ounce package.

Marble Cheesecake Squares

CHOCOLATE TRUFFLE CHEESECAKE

    1 cup chocolate wafer crumbs (approx. 20 wafers)
    3 tablespoons PARKAY Margarine, melted
    2 (8 oz.) pkgs. PHILADELPHIA BRAND Cream Cheese, softened
    ⅔ cup sugar
    2 eggs
    1 cup BAKER'S Semi-Sweet Real Chocolate Chips, melted
    ½ teaspoon vanilla
    Creamy Raspberry Sauce

- Preheat oven to 350°.
- Stir together crumbs and margarine in small bowl; press onto bottom of 9-inch springform pan. Bake 10 minutes.
- Beat cream cheese and sugar in large mixing bowl at medium speed with electric mixer until well blended.
- Add eggs, one at a time, mixing well after each addition.
- Blend in melted chocolate chips and vanilla; pour over crust.
- Bake 45 minutes. Loosen cake from rim of pan; cool before removing rim of pan. Chill.
- Spoon Creamy Raspberry Sauce onto each serving plate. Place slice of cheesecake over sauce. Garnish as desired.   *10 to 12 servings*

CREAMY RASPBERRY SAUCE

    1 (10 oz.) pkg. BIRDS EYE Quick Thaw Red Raspberries in a Lite Syrup, thawed
    3 tablespoons whipping cream

- Place raspberries in food processor or blender container; process until smooth. Strain. Stir in cream.

Prep time: 30 minutes plus chilling
Cooking time: 45 minutes

82

◆ ◆
A dusting of powdered sugar or cocoa is an attractive topping for bar cookies or cheesecakes. Place a paper doily or paper strips over the dessert. Sift powdered sugar onto the dessert just before serving. Carefully remove the doily or paper strips.

COFFEE MOCHA CRUNCH CHEESECAKE

This sophisticated cheesecake combines a crisp crust of chocolate wafers and nuts with a rich mocha cream cheese filling and a delicate coffee creme topping.

    1¼ cups chocolate wafer crumbs (approx. 25 wafers)
    ⅓ cup PARKAY Margarine, melted
    ⅓ cup ground walnuts
    ¼ cup granulated sugar
    1 (8 oz.) pkg. PHILADELPHIA BRAND Cream Cheese, softened
    ½ cup packed brown sugar
    1 (1 oz.) square BAKER'S Unsweetened Chocolate, melted
    2 teaspoons MAXWELL HOUSE Instant Coffee Granules
    1 (16 oz.) container COOL WHIP Whipped Topping, thawed

- Stir together crumbs, margarine, walnuts and granulated sugar in small bowl; press onto bottom and up sides of 9-inch pie plate. Chill.
- Beat cream cheese, brown sugar, chocolate and coffee in large mixing bowl at medium speed with electric mixer until well blended.
- Fold in 3 cups whipped topping; pour over crust. Chill until firm.
- Top with remaining whipped topping.
                 8 servings

Prep time: 25 minutes plus chilling

Chocolate Truffle Cheesecake

RICE PUDDING CHEESECAKE

A new way to serve an old family favorite—as a cheesecake!

    1 cup graham cracker crumbs
    3 tablespoons sugar
    3 tablespoons PARKAY Margarine, melted
    4 (8 oz.) pkgs. PHILADELPHIA BRAND Cream Cheese, softened
    1 cup sugar
    1 tablespoon vanilla
    ½ teaspoon ground cinnamon
    4 eggs
    1½ cups cooked MINUTE Rice
    Lingonberry Sauce

* Preheat oven to 350°.
* Mix together crumbs, 3 tablespoons sugar and margarine in small bowl. Press onto bottom of 9-inch springform pan. Bake 10 minutes.
* Beat cream cheese, 1 cup sugar, vanilla and cinnamon in large mixing bowl at medium speed with electric mixer until well blended.
* Add eggs, one at a time, mixing well after each addition. Stir in rice. Pour over crust.
* Bake 1 hour and 5 minutes. Loosen cake from rim of pan; cool before removing rim of pan. Chill. Serve with Lingonberry Sauce.   *10 to 12 servings*

LINGONBERRY SAUCE

    1 (14.11 oz.) jar lingonberries
    2 tablespoons cold water

* Place lingonberries in food processor or blender container; process until well blended. Strain. Stir in water.

Prep time: 35 minutes plus chilling
Cooking time: 1 hour and 5 minutes

84

MINI ALMOND CHEESECAKES

Have these on hand for those unexpected guests—these cheesecakes can be stored in the freezer up to one month.

    1 cup ground almonds
    2 tablespoons PARKAY Margarine, melted
    1 envelope unflavored gelatin
    ¼ cup cold water
    2 (8 oz.) containers Light PHILADELPHIA BRAND Pasteurized Process Cream Cheese Product
    ¾ cup skim milk
    ½ cup sugar or 12 packets sugar substitute
    ¼ teaspoon almond extract
    3 cups peeled peach slices

* Stir together almonds and margarine in small bowl. Press mixture evenly onto bottoms of twelve paper-lined baking cups.
* Soften gelatin in water in small saucepan; stir over low heat until dissolved.
* Beat cream cheese product, milk, sugar and extract in large mixing bowl at medium speed with electric mixer until well blended. Stir in gelatin. Pour into baking cups; freeze until firm.
* Place peaches in food processor or blender container; process until smooth. Spoon peach purée onto individual plates.
* Remove cheesecakes from freezer 10 minutes before serving. Peel off paper. Invert cheesecakes onto plates. Garnish with additional peach slices, raspberries and fresh mint leaves, if desired.   *12 servings*

Prep time: 20 minutes plus freezing and standing time

Note: For a sweeter peach purée, add sugar to taste.

Mini Almond Cheesecakes

CLASSIC CHEESECAKE

⅓ cup PARKAY Margarine
⅓ cup sugar
1 egg
1¼ cups flour
2 (8 oz.) pkgs. PHILADELPHIA
   BRAND Cream Cheese, softened
½ cup sugar
1 tablespoon lemon juice
1 teaspoon grated lemon peel
½ teaspoon vanilla
3 eggs
1 cup BREAKSTONE'S Sour Cream
1 tablespoon sugar
1 teaspoon vanilla

• Preheat oven to 450°.
• Beat margarine and ⅓ cup sugar in small mixing bowl at medium speed with electric mixer until light and fluffy; blend in one egg. Add flour; mix well.
• Spread dough onto bottom and 1½ inches up sides of 9-inch springform pan. Bake 5 minutes. Remove crust from oven. *Reduce oven temperature to 325°.*
• Beat cream cheese, ½ cup sugar, juice, peel and ½ teaspoon vanilla in large mixing bowl at medium speed with electric mixer until well blended.
• Add eggs, one at a time, mixing well after each addition; pour into crust.
• Bake at 325°, 50 minutes.
• Stir together sour cream, 1 tablespoon sugar and 1 teaspoon vanilla in small bowl. Spread evenly over cake; continue baking 10 minutes. Loosen cake from rim of pan; cool before removing rim of pan. Chill.
• Serve with BIRDS EYE Frozen Quick Thaw Strawberries in Syrup, thawed, if desired.   *10 to 12 servings*

Prep time: 30 minutes plus chilling
Cooking time: 1 hour

86

PEANUTTY HOT FUDGE CHEESECAKE

1½ cups graham cracker crumbs
⅓ cup PARKAY Margarine, melted
¼ cup granulated sugar
1 (8 oz.) pkg. PHILADELPHIA
   BRAND Cream Cheese, softened
1 cup powdered sugar
⅓ cup peanut butter
3 cups thawed COOL WHIP Whipped
   Topping
¼ cup chopped peanuts
¼ cup KRAFT Hot Fudge Topping,
   heated

• Preheat oven to 350°.
• Stir together crumbs, margarine and granulated sugar in small bowl; press onto bottom and ½ inch up sides of 9-inch springform pan. Bake 10 minutes. Cool.
• Beat cream cheese, powdered sugar and peanut butter in large mixing bowl at medium speed with electric mixer until well blended.
• Fold in whipped topping; pour into crust. Sprinkle with peanuts. Chill until firm.
• Carefully remove rim of pan just before serving. Drizzle topping over cheesecake just before serving.   *10 to 12 servings*

Prep time: 15 minutes plus chilling

◆◆◆

You can determine that a cheesecake is done baking when the top has lost its sheen.

To lessen the effect of cracking, allow cheesecake to cool 5 minutes. Insert thin metal spatula between cake or crust and rim of pan; run spatula around inside edge to loosen cake.

Peanutty Hot Fudge Cheesecake

AMARETTO PEACH CHEESECAKE

3 tablespoons PARKAY Margarine
⅓ cup sugar
1 egg
¾ cup flour
3 (8 oz.) pkgs. PHILADELPHIA
    BRAND Cream Cheese, softened
¾ cup sugar
3 tablespoons flour
3 eggs
1 (16 oz.) can peach halves, drained,
    puréed
¼ cup almond-flavored liqueur

- Preheat oven to 450°.
- Beat margarine and ⅓ cup sugar in small bowl at medium speed with electric mixer until light and fluffy. Beat in one egg. Add ¾ cup flour; mix well.
- Spread dough onto bottom of 9-inch springform pan. Bake 10 minutes.
- Beat cream cheese, ¾ cup sugar and 3 tablespoons flour in large mixing bowl at medium speed with electric mixer until well blended.
- Add three eggs, one at a time, mixing well after each addition. Add peaches and liqueur; mix well. Pour over crust.
- Bake 10 minutes. *Reduce oven temperature to 250°.* Continue baking 1 hour and 5 minutes. Loosen cake from rim of pan; cool before removing rim of pan. Chill.   *10 to 12 servings*

Prep time: 25 minutes plus chilling
Cooking time: 1 hour and 15 minutes

CARAMEL BROWNIE CHEESECAKE

1 (8 oz.) pkg. brownie mix
1 egg
1 tablespoon cold water
1 (14 oz.) bag KRAFT Caramels
1 (5 oz.) can evaporated milk
2 (8 oz.) pkgs. PHILADELPHIA
    BRAND Cream Cheese, softened
½ cup sugar
1 teaspoon vanilla
2 eggs
    KRAFT Chocolate Topping

- Preheat oven to 350°.
- Mix together brownie mix, one egg and water in medium bowl until well blended. Spread into greased 9-inch square baking pan. Bake 25 minutes.
- Melt caramels with milk in heavy 1½-quart saucepan over low heat, stirring frequently until smooth. Reserve ⅓ cup caramel mixture for topping. Pour remaining caramel mixture over crust.
- Beat cream cheese, sugar and vanilla in large mixing bowl at medium speed with electric mixer until well blended.
- Add two eggs, one at a time, mixing well after each addition. Pour over caramel mixture in pan.
- Bake 40 minutes; cool. Chill.
- Heat reserved caramel mixture in small saucepan until warm. Spoon over individual servings of cheesecake; drizzle with chocolate topping.
                12 to 16 servings

Prep time: 30 minutes plus chilling
Cooking time: 40 minutes

Variation: Substitute 9-inch springform pan for square baking pan. Loosen cake from rim of pan before cooling.

Microwave Tip: To melt caramels, microwave caramels with milk in small deep glass bowl on HIGH 2½ to 3½ minutes or until sauce is smooth when stirred, stirring after each minute.

88

89

Caramel Brownie Cheesecake

HOLIDAY EGGNOG CHEESECAKE

2 cups vanilla wafer crumbs (approx. 56 wafers)
6 tablespoons PARKAY Margarine, melted
1 teaspoon ground nutmeg
4 (8 oz.) pkgs. PHILADELPHIA BRAND Cream Cheese, softened
1 cup sugar
3 tablespoons flour
3 tablespoons rum
1 teaspoon vanilla
2 eggs
1 cup whipping cream
4 egg yolks

- Preheat oven to 325°.
- Mix together crumbs, margarine and nutmeg in small bowl. Press onto bottom and 1½ inches up sides of 9-inch springform pan. Bake 10 minutes.
- Beat cream cheese, sugar, flour, rum and vanilla in large mixing bowl at medium speed with electric mixer until well blended.
- Add two whole eggs, one at a time, mixing well after each addition. Blend in cream and yolks. Pour into crust.
- Bake 1 hour and 15 minutes. Loosen cake from rim of pan; cool before removing rim of pan. Chill. Sprinkle with additional ground nutmeg, if desired.

10 to 12 servings

Prep time: 20 minutes plus chilling
Cooking time: 1 hour and 15 minutes

CITRUS FRUIT CHEESECAKE

Assorted fresh fruit makes a festive topping for this traditional baked cheesecake with a hint of orange.

1 cup graham cracker crumbs
⅓ cup packed brown sugar
¼ cup PARKAY Margarine, melted
4 (8 oz.) pkgs. PHILADELPHIA BRAND Cream Cheese, softened
1 cup sugar
4 eggs
2 tablespoons grated orange peel
Assorted fresh fruit

- Preheat oven to 325°.
- Stir together crumbs, sugar and margarine in small bowl; press onto bottom of 9-inch springform pan. Bake 10 minutes.
- Beat cream cheese and sugar in large mixing bowl at medium speed with electric mixer until well blended.
- Add eggs, one at a time, mixing well after each addition. Blend in peel; pour over crust.
- Bake 50 minutes.
- Loosen cake from rim of pan; cool before removing rim of pan. Chill.
- Top with fruit. Garnish with lime zest, if desired. *10 to 12 servings*

Prep time: 20 minutes plus chilling
Cooking time: 50 minutes

◆◆◆

Star fruit or carambola is a natural beauty. Its flavors range from slightly tart to sweet. Select firm, shiny fruit and allow to ripen at room temperature. Browning along the edges is a sign of ripening. Slice crosswise to form stars; do not peel.

Citrus Fruit Cheesecake

S'MORE CHEESECAKE

1¼ cups graham cracker crumbs
⅓ cup PARKAY Margarine, melted
¼ cup sugar
1 (12 oz.) container PHILADELPHIA
  BRAND Soft Cream Cheese
5 (1.45 ozs. each) milk chocolate candy
  bars, melted
1 (1.45 ozs. each) milk chocolate candy
  bar, finely chopped
1 cup KRAFT Miniature Marshmallows
1½ cups thawed COOL WHIP Whipped
  Topping

- Stir together crumbs, margarine and sugar in small bowl; press onto bottom and 1 inch up sides of 9-inch springform pan.
- Stir together cream cheese and melted chocolate in small bowl until well blended; pour into crust. Sprinkle with chopped chocolate.
- Fold marshmallows into whipped topping; spread over cheesecake. Chill.

10 to 12 servings

Prep time: 15 minutes plus chilling

APPLESAUCE LEMON CHEESECAKE

1 cup gingersnap cookie crumbs
  (approx. 15 cookies)
¼ cup PARKAY Margarine, melted
3 (8 oz.) pkgs. PHILADELPHIA
  BRAND Cream Cheese, softened
⅔ cup sugar
3 tablespoons flour
3 eggs
1 cup applesauce
½ teaspoon grated lemon peel

- Preheat oven to 350°.
- Mix together crumbs and margarine in small bowl. Press onto bottom of 9-inch springform pan. Bake 10 minutes.
- Beat cream cheese, sugar and flour in large mixing bowl at medium speed with electric mixer until well blended.
- Add eggs, one at a time, mixing well after each addition. Blend in applesauce and peel. Pour over crust.
- Bake 1 hour and 15 minutes. Loosen cake from rim of pan; cool before removing rim of pan. Chill. *10 to 12 servings*

Prep time: 25 minutes plus chilling
Cooking time: 1 hour and 15 minutes

BANANA CHOCOLATE MINI CHEESECAKES

12 creme-filled chocolate cookies
1 (8 oz.) pkg. PHILADELPHIA
  BRAND Cream Cheese, softened
⅓ cup sugar
1 teaspoon lemon juice
2 eggs
½ cup mashed ripe banana
2 ozs. BAKER'S GERMAN'S Sweet
  Chocolate, broken into pieces
1½ tablespoons cold water
1½ tablespoons PARKAY Margarine
  Banana slices

- Preheat oven to 350°.
- Place one cookie onto bottom of each of twelve paper-lined muffin cups.
- Beat cream cheese, sugar and juice in large mixing bowl at medium speed with electric mixer until well blended.
- Add eggs, one at a time, mixing well after each addition. Blend in mashed banana; pour over cookies, filling each cup ¾ full.
- Bake 15 to 20 minutes or until set.
- Melt chocolate with water in small saucepan over low heat, stirring constantly. Remove from heat; stir in margarine until melted. Cool.
- Top cheesecakes with banana slices just before serving; drizzle with chocolate sauce. *12 servings*

Prep time: 15 minutes
Cooking time: 20 minutes

92

ALMOND BRICKLE CHEESECAKE

      1 cup shortbread cookie crumbs
        (approx. 15 cookies)
      3 tablespoons PARKAY Margarine,
        melted
      1 tablespoon granulated sugar
      3 (8 oz.) pkgs. PHILADELPHIA
        BRAND Cream Cheese, softened
      ⅔ cup granulated sugar
      ½ teaspoon vanilla
      3 eggs
      ½ cup BREAKSTONE'S Sour Cream
      1 (6 oz.) pkg. almond brickle chips
      1 tablespoon flour
      1 cup crushed shortbread cookies
        (approx. 13 cookies)
      ⅓ cup packed brown sugar
      ¼ cup PARKAY Margarine
      1 cup chopped almonds
      ¼ cup KRAFT Caramel Topping

- Preheat oven to 350°.
- Mix together 1 cup crumbs, 3 tablespoons margarine and 1 tablespoon granulated sugar in small bowl. Press onto bottom of 9-inch springform pan. Bake 10 minutes.
- Beat cream cheese, ⅔ cup granulated sugar and vanilla in large mixing bowl at medium speed with electric mixer until well blended.
- Add eggs, one at a time, mixing well after each addition. Blend in sour cream.
- Toss together chips with flour in small bowl; stir into cream cheese mixture. Pour over crust.
- Mix together 1 cup crushed cookies and brown sugar; cut in ¼ cup margarine until mixture resembles coarse crumbs. Stir in almonds. Sprinkle over cream cheese mixture.
- Bake 1 hour and 5 minutes. Drizzle with caramel topping. Continue baking 10 minutes. Loosen cake from rim of pan; cool before removing rim of pan. Chill.

10 to 12 servings

Prep time: 30 minutes plus chilling
Cooking time: 1 hour and 15 minutes

PEANUT BUTTER CHOCOLATE CHEESECAKE

      1 cup graham cracker crumbs
      ½ cup finely chopped peanuts
      ⅓ cup PARKAY Margarine, melted
      2 tablespoons sugar
      3 (8 oz.) pkgs. PHILADELPHIA
        BRAND Cream Cheese, softened
      ¾ cup sugar
      2 tablespoons flour
      1 teaspoon vanilla
      3 eggs
      5 (1.8 ozs. each) pkgs. milk chocolate
        peanut butter cups, chopped
        (approx. 1½ cups)
      1 tablespoon flour

- Preheat oven to 325°.
- Mix together crumbs, peanuts, margarine and 2 tablespoons sugar in small bowl. Press onto bottom and 1½ inches up sides of 9-inch springform pan. Bake 10 minutes.
- Beat cream cheese, ¾ cup sugar, 2 tablespoons flour and vanilla in large mixing bowl at medium speed with electric mixer until well blended.
- Add eggs, one at a time, mixing well after each addition.
- Toss together chopped peanut butter cups with 1 tablespoon flour in small bowl. Stir into cream cheese mixture. Pour into crust.
- Bake 1 hour. Loosen cake from rim of pan; cool before removing rim of pan. Chill.

10 to 12 servings

Prep time: 20 minutes plus chilling
Cooking time: 1 hour

Index

96